PRAISE FOR
RIDE OR DIE

"I've never read a book that gives us as much as *Ride or Die* gives us. This miracle of a book challenges, affirms, heals, reveals, and loves like nothing I've ever come across before. Shanita Hubbard has opened herself to us all for the purpose of asking us to be better to and for the people around us. She is one of our preeminent master teachers, using hip-hop as her curriculum, and we are all better for having been given these lessons."

—David Dennis Jr., author of
The Movement Made Us

"Shanita masterfully navigates the complexities of Black womanhood through hip-hop's problematic lens—as only a thought leader of her caliber can. As such, *Ride or Die* is much more than 'a feminist manifesto'; it's an impassioned testimony that implores each of us to reassess our participation in—and contributions to—the continuous destruction of Black women."

—Jay Connor, Senior Editor,
Culture & Entertainment at *The Root*

RIDE OR DIE

A Feminist Manifesto
for the Well-Being of
Black Women

SHANITA HUBBARD

LEGACY
LIT

NEW YORK · BOSTON

Legacy Lit, an imprint of Grand Central Publishing
Hachette Book Group
1290 Avenue of the Americas
New York, NY 10104
LegacyLitBooks.com
Twitter.com/LegacyLitBooks
Instagram.com/LegacyLitBooks

First Edition: November 2022

Grand Central Publishing is a division of Hachette Book Group, Inc. The Legacy Lit and Grand Central Publishing names and logos are trademarks of Hachette Book Group, Inc.

The Hachette Speakers Bureau provides a wide range of authors for speaking events. To find out more, go to www.hachettespeakersbureau.com or call (866) 376-6591.

The publisher is not responsible for websites (or their content) that are not owned by the publisher.

Library of Congress Cataloging-in-Publication Data

Names: Hubbard, Shanita, author.
Title: Ride-or-die : a feminist manifesto for the well-being of Black women / Shanita Hubbard.
Description: First edition. | New York, NY : Legacy Lit, 2022. | Includes bibliographical references. | Summary: "Cultural criticism and pop culture history intertwine to dissect how hip hop has sidelined Black women's identity and emotional well-being." —Provided by publisher.
Identifiers: LCCN 2022019787 (print) | LCCN 2022019788 (ebook) | ISBN 9780306874673 (hardcover) | ISBN 9780306874666 (ebook)
Subjects: LCSH: Women, Black—Psychology. | African American women—Psychology. | Women, Black—Race identity. | African American women—Race identity. | Hip-hop—Social aspects. | Hip-hop—Psychological aspects.
Classification: LCC HQ1163 .H83 2022 (print) | LCC HQ1163 (ebook) | DDC 305.48/896—dc23/eng/20220511
LC record available at https://lccn.loc.gov/2022019787
LC ebook record available at https://lccn.loc.gov/2022019788

ISBNs: 9780306874673 (hardcover); 9780306874666 (ebook)

Printed in the United States of America

LSC-C

Printing 1, 2022

For Jordyn, Mommy, and Nanny—
this book only exists because of what you three
have given me.

The love expressed between women is particular and powerful because we have had to love in order to live; love has been our survival.

—Audre Lorde

CONTENTS

INTRODUCTION

AN ODE TO BLACK WOMEN

Honey, Sadie Oliver's seven daughters are not to be played with. My nanny raised the women who showed me that unconditional support and love could give a person wings. I was never afraid to fall when I took a leap because I knew the Black women in my life would swoop in and use every resource they had to ensure I stayed in flight. I grew up surrounded by Black women who led families, nurtured communities, and raised some of the most brilliant people I've ever met. My courage came from knowing that they were my supporters.

I knew the Black women in my life were my superpower when I was twenty-two years old and had an anxiety attack while I was traveling.

During my last year of graduate school I decided to enroll in a study abroad program. The program required me to live with a Spanish-speaking host family in a small town located just outside Madrid, Spain. Prior to that I had only traveled domestically with friends or family. Traveling with family felt safest because I was literally moving around with my foundation. In 1979, the year I was born, my family started annual family reunions. My aunts and grandmother birthed these highly organized trips for hundreds of people. They didn't have the privilege of our technology to make it more efficient. There were no mass emails. There were no Facebook pages to dispense information on hotels and activities, no apps to send money for payments, or Zoom links to have family meetings to discuss the logistics. It was just a handful of Black women coordinating in different states by sending letters in the mail and making phone calls to make sure the family connections and love for each other remained fully intact despite our geographical distance. Every summer my grandmother and aunts would charter a fifty-person passenger van and my family from all parts of New York would meet in Yonkers so we could ride together to visit our family in North Carolina for the weekend. The whole bus would smell like fried chicken. All the kids were high on sugar and our laughter bounced off the walls of the bus. We knew better than to run around. My cousins, brothers, and I would all cram together in a few rows and trade secrets, jokes, and snacks for hours. I don't think any of us actually fell asleep; it's more like our bodies would eventually just crash when the sugar and dopamine highs ended. I'm sure the grown-ups were intoxicated on more than sugar and happiness. I'm sure there were a few sips of Pink Champale for my mom and aunties and a little Colt 45 for my uncles. When I went back to grab more food or snacks, the joy from my older relatives was almost palpable. I didn't realize this at the time but those annual family reunions shaped core pieces of who I am. Thanks to my family I grew up knowing that Black women have the ingenuity, love, tenacity, and commitment to always show up for those we love.

This deep-rooted understanding was my focal point as I centered myself on the flight to Spain when I was twenty-two. I decided to travel alone rather than with the group of grad students who were leaving from the States because the flight they selected was too expensive for me. This meant I left the United States for the first time armed with faith, hood Spanglish, the address for my host family, and $1,500 from my student refund check. I started to think about these details on the flight. In Yonkers my broken Spanish mixed with English worked well, but I knew it wouldn't get me far in Spain. I thought about how the European exchange rate would ensure that my little budget wouldn't last long once I arrived. It was 2002 so my plan to go from the airport to my host family's house didn't include Google Maps; I would have to rely on the local taxi drivers. Suddenly things started to feel shaky. What the hell had I gotten myself into? This was a shitty plan. You're not gonna make it and this isn't safe. My sweaty grip clung to the armrest and it felt like there was a rubber band tightening around my lungs. The harder I tried to breathe the tighter it got. I started to gasp. I felt like my heart was beating loud enough for the entire flight to hear. Tears escaped my tightly sealed eyelids. I peeled my sweaty shirt off. The air-conditioned plane felt like a freezer as I sat in my wet tank top. "Are you okay?" the white guy in the window seat to my left whispered to me. "Honey should I get you some help?" the white woman sitting to my right asked. I couldn't open my eyes but I could feel them staring at me. In the middle seat, I felt trapped by them. I shook my head no. I didn't understand what was happening so I had no clue what help would even look like. As the rubber band around my lungs tightened I allowed myself to sink into my fears and imagine how my terrifying fictitious scenarios could possibly play out. If my money runs out I'll call my mom or aunts. If I get mugged at the airport on the way to my host family's house I'll call my mom collect if I have to. If I don't feel safe with my host family I'll grab my bags, find a pay phone, and call my mom and aunts and they will pool their money and get me on the first flight out of there. No matter how farfetched or extreme I allowed my thoughts to go, they always landed on the inevitable: the Black women in my life would protect me. The more I settled into that thought the calmer I became. My breathing became effortless, my heartbeat normalized, and I felt safe enough to open my eyes.

Twenty years later and the reality that Black women will always show up for me still allows me to breathe. Whether that fear is stemming from leaving the country for three months, or publishing my first book, I know with complete certainty that I am fully supported in life.

I am who I am because of other Black women so I wrote this book to focus on us and our well-being. When I was younger I used to read Susan Taylor's monthly column in *Essence*. She wrote about the inner lives of Black women in a way that fed my soul. Since then I dreamed of writing a book that would make Black women feel seen. *Ride or Die* is a conversation starter for Black women about contemporary topics that are essential for the world we live in today: a world where hip-hop is now the dominant musical genre and a global phenomenon. I grew up a hip-hop head, and artist like Nas, Jay-Z, the Notorious B.I.G., and Kiss were my writing inspirations. All writers love good storytelling and strong word play. These dudes use their words to skillfully craft vignettes about the lives of Black men in our communities. They masterfully pull listeners into their stories and leave us feeling a deeper connection to the world. But the older I got the more I started to realize that far too often the lives of Black women were either reduced, misrepresented, or missing altogether from hip-hop. I can no longer hear "One Love" by Nas without thinking about the various ways his story about incarceration neglected the unique perspectives of Black women. How has the missing narrative about Black women's lives shaped my perspective as a Black woman? I wrote these pages to speak to areas of Black women's inner lives and experiences that hip-hop has yet to reach and to do what generations of Black women have done for me: give me wings.

1

RIDE OR DIE

We struggle together with Black men against racism, while we also struggle with Black men about sexism.

—The Combahee River Collective
Statement

When the song "Ryde or Die, Bitch" by the LOX was released in 1999, it became a guide for the type of woman I wanted to be. I was twenty-one years old, and this song was both an anthem in hip-hop and a personal road map. I wanted to be seen as a "ride-or-die" chick in the most romantic way. I wanted to be the "Bonnie" to a "Clyde," a beautiful woman who was happily in an "us against the world" relationship. She was celebrated and highly valued in the music that I loved the most—hip-hop. She was renowned for the sacrifices she made for her partner at almost any cost to herself. She was valued for her love and loyalty through the labor of it all.

The ride-or-die chick is synonymous with some of our foremothers who love our families deeply, but never learned the delicate balance of loving others while protecting their own emotional needs. They taught us how to keep our family close, how to preserve family traditions, and how to raise brilliant Black girls who will grow to be amazing Black women. She is the person fully willing to do all the heavy lifting for those she loves. She is also the one who sacrificed pieces of herself for her family, like planning all the family events and arriving first and leaving last to ensure all the cleaning is done. She modeled how we should give every single ounce of ourselves as Black women, or else we couldn't call it love. That we should give as much as we could—of our heart, time, energy. The ride-or-die chick has always been fully present in my life and in the Black community. She comes in different forms, too, and appears in all types of places. Of course, she's omnipresent—that's her role. She's in our church passing out Bible verses to heal us. She's up in our relationships. She's the model of how we mother. We replicate her in our careers, pouring all that we've learned from her into boardrooms and spaces that don't even know who she is or why she is.

The familiarity is what helps us connect so much to the ride-or-die archetype. It became widely popular in hip-hop because she represents the struggle, the love, and the indomitable survival. It was the lead single from the LOX's second album, *We Are the Streets*. It features hip-hop legends like producer Timbaland and rapper Eve. According to Billboard, it was the most commercially successful single of the famous album. Most importantly, it's a song that provided a label for women, a label that has stuck for more than twenty years.

The song starts with:

I need a ryde or die bitch
I like to rock Prada suits and my ass is fat

The song doesn't make you work too hard for clarity. It spares us the need for intellects to gather and unpack the genius of this song. Jadakiss, the member of the LOX who single-handedly defeated the group Dipset in one of hip-hop's most talked about *Verzuz* battles of 2021, is a lyrical maverick, but this is not a song of substance. It's not an important song. It's not a good song. It's just a song with a beat. In fact, it's not even a song that deserves to be written about, except that it provides a visual representation of a "ride-or-die" chick. Let's be clear. The ride-or-die chick has existed since the beginning of time. She's like your mother's mother and her mother, and so on. She predates rap. But what the LOX did was box her up all neat and nice and serve us her description. They provide her description in the opening. After they tell us what she looks like, they then provide the job requirements, should you choose to apply to be a ride-or-die chick—which I did, and was employed as one for a large portion of my life. Many Black women have been applicants.

Like most actual job descriptions, there are a list of

duties for being a ride or die. The LOX and Timbaland break it down in an extreme circumstance, but still, it teaches us the basics: She has a willingness to literally kill for her man. She'll do a lot more than just visit her man when he's locked up—that type of support would only be basic. A ride-or-die chick does so MUCH more. Oh, and when she's not visiting, she's transporting coke out of town for him and killing his enemies and using her fake credit card twice in the store for him. Or as Jadakiss suggests, *Make her use a fake credit card twice in a store / Might make you do it tomorrow, you triflin' whore.*

Sure, the lyrics themselves are hyperbole, but this was a summertime anthem, and it's a classic concept ingrained in our culture. The fact that we never questioned how Eve could be in the chorus of a song that's about women performing this kind of labor is fitting. It's symbolic of the way some Black women can internalize and perpetuate the ride-or-die mentality. Some Black women sing this proverbial chorus daily. I'm guilty of this too. My family comprises mostly women. The majority of the women in my family are financially self-sufficient, employed, and rarely struggle with housing insecurity. We know how to "make a dollar out of fifteen cents." We can get creative with a budget, keep an emergency fund, and figure out a way to keep the lights on. When one of the men in my family fails to operate at the same level, we'll sit around and pray. *Lord, he just needs a good Black woman by his side.* Conversely, if one of the women stumbles, the same prayer circle will gather, but instead it's *Lord, help her find a way.*

I have a thirty-four-year-old cousin, Fred, who is one of the smartest people I've ever met. He processes information in a way that's just beautiful to witness. He's analytical, quick-witted, and thinks deeply about the world around him. My family and I always imagined he would be an engineer, doctor, or whatever profession that demanded advanced intelligence. Fred went to Columbia University. His dad ensured Fred had a college fund and never lacked for anything while he attended college. He probably had no idea where the financial aid office was located on campus, or a clue about what his monthly rent or car payment cost. His dad handled it for him. He decided to take a break from college one semester. After five years, we figured this was less of a break and more of a departure. He's now a sales associate at the Gap. He loves it, and I'm sure he does well. Yet I still find myself wanting him to pursue a profession where his full potential can be realized. When I worry that he won't, I reassure myself with *"He's handsome, sweet, and loving. One day he'll meet a good Black woman that will help him get where he needs to be. She'll put that work in and get him together."*

I've always viewed other Black women as the "cure" for whatever was "broken," especially with the men in our family. My cousin James was the guy who could walk into a room and effortlessly command attention. He was funny, charismatic, and charming. Holiday events never felt the same until he arrived. When he walked in the door at Nanny's house on Christmas, it felt like a Black episode of *Cheers*. "*Ayyyyyyyyyyye,*" we shouted in unison. He leaned into his role as the center of the event. He cracked his flawless smile, hugged the aunties, and dapped up the uncles. Five minutes in, the entire room was as loud with laughter as a comedy club. He could always find a way to liven up the mood. He eventually became addicted to drugs. Addiction is a thief, and it doesn't care what it steals. It stole his magnetic personality, his charm, and charisma. He became volatile. It was impossible to be around him because of the fear of sparking his rage. I would tell the aunties, "If he had a good sista that understood his potential, none of this would've ever happened to him. She would've worked with him." The chorus would join me: "Girl, I know."

The ride-or-die chick is woven into our family dynamics, in our music, and she's the foundation of the spaces we hold dearest. The LOX might have popularized the ride-or-die title and young people in the hood may help keep the name relevant, but the blueprint of her creation was crafted by our grandparents in the Black church. The song tells us that she rocks icy chains, has an earring in her tongue, and her man's name tattooed on her neck. In church, her aesthetics may be different, but her characteristics are the same. Under the big hats, long skirts, stockings, and clutched pearls lies the architect of the ride-or-die chick.

The ride-or-die chick in the Black church is silent, loyal, and forgiving, even of a perpetually unfaithful husband—it doesn't matter if that husband is the pastor. "Forgive as the Lord forgave you" and "love covers a multitude of sins" will be some of her favorite verses to share with you during a challenge. The ride-or-die chick doesn't only manifest in church via the endless forgiveness of perpetually unfaithful men, her other attribute is that she's silent about her pain. "The Lord will fight for you, and you have only to be silent" (Exodus 14:14). It's a passage to help ensure women remain silent about their pain while they continue to perform the labor needed to keep the daily operations flowing. Which she does without fail. It's clear to Sister Ride or Die that the burden of humankind should always be a woman's to carry. She cleans the church, cooks the meals for fundraisers, and creates and prints the church programs. She does this all without financial compensation. All in an act of service "unto the Lord." Oh, and she teaches Sunday school too.

Her labor is occasionally affirmed in the church when she receives thanks from the pulpit by the pastor and approving nods from the congregation.

As Black women, no matter what our religious or spiritual beliefs, our lives have been affected by Sister Ride or Die because Christianity is a dominant belief system of our society. Therefore the question is, are these women, Sister Ride or Dies, giving out free labor in the name of God, or is this an example of the Black church upholding systems of patriarchy similar to the men in hip-hop? Both. A lot of these Black women, especially older ones, are in fact laboring in church as a form of ministry. As a service to God. But it's not uncommon for this service to be manipulated, expected, and taken for granted by the male leadership in the church. And as much as we take our cues from the church in this country, we take them from hip-hop too. There are a lot of similarities that these two spaces have in common that don't work well for Black women.

Patriarchy in the Black church cannot be divorced from racism in the United States, nor can it be viewed separately from the ways they manifest in hip-hop. The first Black church was formed in 1773—fourteen years before the three-fifths compromise in the constitution was ratified.

While Black men were treated as three-fifths of a white man everywhere in the country, in the Black church they were not just men—they were "men of God" who had "spiritual authority" to rule. It was one of the few spaces where this leadership could not only be possible, but could also remain unquestioned. This unquestioned, "God-ordained" authority often resulted in abuse that harmed an even less powerful group—Black women in the church. It was modeled in homes and communities for generations. This is not to diminish the important role the Black church played in our communities. Multiple things can be true at the same time and criticism doesn't mean contempt. The Black church served as a cornerstone for the civil rights movement and offers a space where Black people can grow spiritually and provide social services to communities. It is also a space where patriarchy roars unchecked—sometimes "in the name of God," and sometimes in the name of "letting a man be a man" in a country that still treats him as less than one. "Let a man be a man" is a common phrase that serves as a response to making a decision from a position of leadership, even if he doesn't have the range or experience to do so. When I heard an elder Black man say this to a woman in church one day, she nodded in agreement. We often capitulate as a way to validate men. Which in itself is a deeply flawed behavior. Nevertheless, there is no separation of church and hood. The elders of the church are the pillars in our community. They run Black homes and raise Black families while modeling and echoing these same notions we hear amplified in our music using different language.

An uneven distribution of labor and viewing love through labor are core concepts of the ride-or-die chick. While she's fully present in the Black church, these same attributes are fully present in Black women in general, even those who have never stepped foot inside a sanctuary. Labor as love is consistently our model in Black culture; we internalize it and donate that perspective to those we raise. It becomes a generational burden. When this kind of love paradigm is modeled by our foremothers and forefathers, this becomes the baseline for how we understand romantic relationships. Which is why almost every Black married woman I know works full-time and still handles the majority of the domestic work in the home while the household bills are evenly split. Apparently only bills are gender neutral.

It can take a long time to recognize toxic generational patterns. It can take even longer to admit when you're the one keeping the cycle going.

One of my favorite things is Black family traditions. On New Year's Eve our homes need to be spotless before midnight strikes. A clean house at midnight means your home will be in order all year. A messy house means a chaotic house all year. This is just a superstition, but it's harmless and makes me feel good.

In December of 2019 I was ready to take my chance with chaos. About two weeks before Christmas I forced myself to stay up to two a.m. to wrap my daughter's gifts. She didn't believe in Santa but I believe in surprises. I waited until my then nine-year-old was fully asleep to dig out her gifts from the places I hid them. My daughter and I lived alone so I knew I would have all the uninterrupted time I needed. I dug around my large bedroom closet for about three minutes without finding her laptop and L.O.L. Surprise dolls. I stepped out of the closet and realized that I was exhausted; I sat on the floor in my bedroom and considered just telling Jordyn Christmas is canceled this year. I was sick of searching. After about five minutes I went back into the closet for round two. *Why the hell can't I find her damn gifts?* I grunted as I threw a pair of tall, black knee-high boots. As soon as I spit the words out the answer fell off the hangers. A row of sundresses landed on my shoulder. I slammed them on the floor like they were secretly hiding her presents from me. Why the hell are these summer clothes still in my closet in December? This is crazy. My house is too unorganized. Teaching three college classes, writing one-thousand-word articles for publications, cooking dinner, and googling third-grade common core math occupied most of my weekdays. On Saturdays when my daughter is with my mom, I usually recharge by meeting up with friends or watching TV and relaxing. Sunday nights are for uninterrupted time with my child and preparation for the week. I stared aimlessly into the closet, mentally recapping my daily routine in search for a time when I could reorganize my closet. The only thing I could do was eliminate my downtime on Saturdays. I sighed and negotiated with myself. *All you need is one Saturday afternoon to declutter your house and reorganize.* I stopped the negotiations. I could afford to probably just hire somebody to do it but there I was, negotiating the one single slot I had left in my life for myself. To even think about hiring somebody was completely embarrassing. No one was listening to my thoughts but I was ashamed. I was completely physically capable of doing it myself despite how exhausted I was; why would I even think of something like that? It felt like I was letting somebody else do my job as a mother. My closing argument to myself was: your mother was a single mom of three who worked TWO full-time jobs, attended all your school activities, stayed on top of your homework, and never had to hire anyone to help her in the house. Nanny raised eight kids alone after

Grandad died. She wouldn't even dream of hiring help. Women in your family don't do that. We're good mothers. My decision to deprioritize my downtime and stay on top of my ride-or-die game to make room for more labor was solidified in that moment. I then realized that I had left the gifts at my mom's house so I wouldn't have to hide them. I stepped over the mess I'd made and went to bed, realizing as I snuggled my pillow that I would need more than one Saturday to organize the closet and bring more order into my life.

In professional settings, the ride-or-die mentality manifests a little differently. In our homes, it's about showing love to our family by pushing beyond healthy limits. At work, the ride-or-die chick pushes herself without establishing limits as a way to show her company she can handle anything. She's the sister that will always stay late, work though her lunch, and rarely take vacations. *"I've only used personal time off from work three times in five years. I even forgot the process for requesting time off,"* she'll say with hidden pride.

The ride-or-die chick is separate from the sister who overperforms out of fear of losing her job, financial pressure, or even just trying to make it within a world where capitalism rules everything around her. The ride or die at work isn't necessarily motivated by money. It's more about proving her abilities and worth to her supervisors and peers. She will handle any task that's asked of her, despite how far removed it is from her job description. She *needs* to prove her loyalty, abilities, and worth, so she overperforms. She's willing to prove this through labor and call it ambition, despite being worked like a mule and rewarded like a peasant. Her boss may never say "I need a ride-or-die employee." He doesn't know the secret to her cape. Either way, the ride or die lives on.

It's easy to share stories about the ride-or-die chicks I've met. It takes no emotional labor for me to take inventory of the professional work mules I know or see in myself. The hard work comes with taking inventory of how the ride-or-die chick plays out in our romantic relationships.

The LOX's song "Ryde or Die, Bitch" outlines extreme examples that could serve as a shield against any real self-assessment of my role in this archetype. I never had sex with a man on a jail visit. I never stole a credit card to take him shopping. I never even considered killing anyone for my man, let alone doing it. I never went through such lengths to show my love. But really though, the ride-or-die chick lives in me, and nobody ever had to summon her by name, she just showed up because she's ingrained in me.

During my twenties, she would appear faster if I fell in love with the type of brother I grew up conditioned to protect: the "endangered Black man" fighting against a criminal system that has always been anything but "just."

When I was twenty-four years old, I moved from Ohio back to Yonkers, New York, after receiving a master's degree in criminal justice at Bowling Green State University. I had the right degree in the wrong city. Ideally, living anywhere close to New York City with a master of science in criminal justice should have made my job prospects plentiful. New York is full of agencies centered around prison reform, which was my specific interest in criminal justice. Reality and idealism never met. In reality, attending undergrad in South Carolina and grad school in Ohio meant I had no professional contacts outside of the states I'd matriculated in. I had done my internships outside of New York, so I moved back to my hometown with an impressive degree in one hand, a thin resume in the other, and careful plans to make it all work.

I found a job at a community-based organization in Brooklyn. The organization had nothing to do with my larger passion, but my plan included building my network and gaining more professional skills, so I quickly accepted the position. My job was to connect underserved families with resources in the community. I went to work and completed tasks like helping underemployed families find affordable health care, while I made about $790 every two weeks.

I commuted for a total of three hours a day from my house in Mount Vernon to the Flatbush section of Brooklyn. I rented a beautiful, well-maintained large house just outside of Yonkers with my cousins Nellie, Vonnie, and Tonia. We affectionately call each other our soul mates because of our bond. Our four-way bond is forever—like that of two soul mates. My share of the rent was $600 a month. My portion of the utilities and grocery bill averaged $250 a month. I could barely pay that, but I knew there were few comparable places I could afford to live. Even in 2004, living in New York was expensive, which made roommates a requirement for me—something I found shameful at that age. Nevertheless, if I had to live with anyone in the world, I was happy it was with those three women. Sharing a house with my soul mates was fun. Nellie would cook, while the four of us stood in our large kitchen and played the *Destiny Fulfilled* album on repeat. Tonia, Vonnie, and I would take turns singing "Is She the Reason" loud and off-key into a fake microphone. Nellie has a beautiful singing voice, so she would join us for as long as she could tolerate it. I never imagined having roommates again after college. I assumed I would be self-sufficient enough to live alone. Once again, reality and idealism didn't meet. We were in the early stages of our careers and none of us were making a lot of money, so we had a housewarming to help us acquire some essentials. The four of us went to Bed Bath & Beyond to select our registry. The sales assistant helping us asked if we lived in "some type of sorority house." I hoped my exaggerated laughter hid my embarrassment.

My life felt like I was living in a long dark tunnel, chiseling my way out with a steak knife. There were glimpses of light that would permeate the darkness. I had a job I enjoyed but it came with a barely livable salary. I had a great place and lived with people I loved, but my commute to work was brutal. I wasn't making professional connections or moving closer to a career in prison reform. I had to fight to feel moments of joy. I tried to focus on the small and large blessings. It's one hell of a fight when you're broke—but being broke and educated made every blow land harder. I thought I had followed the proverbial equation for success. Two degrees, minus children before marriage were supposed to equal financial success. My life wasn't adding up.

One morning, when I was standing at the bus stop on my way to work, I met a guy who would eventually make my fight for joy a lot easier. We locked eyes when he drove by in a white late model BMW. It wasn't that *standing at the bus stop sucking on a lollipop* moment LL Cool J had rapped about in "Around the Way Girl." I wasn't casually enjoying a summer afternoon in NYC. I was holding my hood on my head with one hand, clutching a huge laptop bag with the other, battling the brutal January winds, and rolling my eyes every five minutes because my bus was late. This meant I would be late for my connecting train. He caught me in between eye rolls. He did a U-turn, parked across the street from the bus, and walked over to me, smiling. He was about six foot one, with a muscular build and smooth brown skin that was interrupted by a long scar across his chin. He wore a beige hoodie, blue jeans, and construction Timbs. I've always been attracted to men who look like they have about two tablespoonsful of hood in them, so he was just my type. His name was Anthony, and he asked me if I wanted a ride. I interrupted his generosity with "I don't know you."

"But I'd like to get to know you. Can I call you tonight?" Anthony asked. I gave him my number. His face lit up when he smiled. I smiled too.

"Glad I could make you smile," he said proudly.

"You didn't, my bus is finally coming." I walked by him and practically ran onto the bus. When I sat down, I could see him standing near his car watching me with that same bright smile on his face. It didn't take long for my smile to catch up to his.

Things moved quickly and naturally between Anthony and me. The initial phone call was followed by a dinner date the next night. Five consecutive dates nights later, and we were having quiet nights at his place. I was spending fewer nights singing in the kitchen with my soul mates and more time in Anthony's living room relaxing while he cooked for me. After only four months of dating, we were already emotionally connected. Anthony was seven years older than me and reminded me of the older guys in my family—all perceptive and all caring. "You've been reading that book all week. It must be good," he said one night while handing me a sample of the spaghetti he was still perfecting in the kitchen. He leaned against the off-white living room wall and waited.

"Yeah, it's a collection of Nikki Giovanni poems from 1968 to 1998," I responded before tasting the food and giving him my nod of approval. "I love this book," I said. I explained that I had borrowed it from a coworker and was rushing to finish it so I could return it. I started to read him a poem called "Ego Tripping."

I lasted three seconds before he busted out laughing. "I'm sorry, but this just feels like a fake-ass *Love Jones* movie," he said as he sat down on the sofa next to me.

"Then leave me alone and let me read in peace," I said, playfully pushing him off his black leather sofa.

He started to walk back into the kitchen, paused, and turned back to me. "You shouldn't have to borrow things you love," he said, "and your mornings shouldn't be so rushed that you forget the things you need."

I was happy that he noticed these little details about my life—it made me feel taken care of.

The next morning, I jumped out of bed and immediately started to panic when I noticed the time. It was already 7:00 a.m. I thought I had slept through the alarm, which meant I would miss my bus and a 9:30 a.m. work meeting. "I turned off the alarm clock," Anthony said as he walked into the bedroom already wearing his standard black sweats and T-shirt he wore when he had to do a lot of work on a car. "I'll drop you off at work in the mornings now. I hired someone to hold things down in the shop. Now you can sleep later without having to rush." He handed me a brand-new copy of the Nikki Giovanni book I was reading and walked out the room. I smiled the whole time as I got ready for work that morning.

Every night with Anthony felt fresh. The tunnel became brighter. We never had the typical "what are we?" discussion. We just knew. Five months after meeting he gave me a key to his apartment. Seven months later it felt like I'd known him all my life.

I was in love and wanted forever with him. He loved

me too, but our forever was put into question eight months into our relationship. Something began to feel off. One night our usual dinner talk was tense. We were both sitting at the same kitchen table but he wasn't there. The blank wall behind me demanded his full attention for the first five minutes of dinner. He barely blinked or moved. He just stared at the wall. "When are you going to tell me what's wrong?" I finally asked. He jumped as if my voice startled him. I searched his face for answers but found none. His face was devoid of emotion. He looked frozen. He lowered his head and my heart raced. He closed his eyes. "I'm going to prison," he said.

The words fell off his lips and snatched the air from my body. We'd shared so much with each other, I thought I knew everything about him, at least the important things. I knew the story behind the scar on his chin and the ones on his heart. He'd told me about the years he spent selling drugs when he was younger, and how he'd been incarcerated for it. My brain started racing. The worst-case scenarios rushed to my brain. *He must have been living a double life behind my back; he'd been selling drugs in the streets while I thought he was busy managing his auto repair shop.*

He read the anger on my face and gently touched my hand. "It's for something I did years before we met," he said. "When I was twenty-six I blew my bail in Virginia."

I could barely concentrate on the words coming out of his mouth but attempted to listen. "I was on trial for selling drugs and I was out on bail. I knew the trial wasn't going my way, so I just packed up my apartment in VA, moved back to NY like nothing happened, and started my life over. The case is still open and now there is an additional charge for jumping bail."

With a degree in criminal justice, I knew exactly what it meant to "blow bail" and how that impacts the original charge, but Anthony nervously gave me these details anyway. He didn't have to search my face hard to know what I thought. I had a lot to say. "Why are you just telling me this now? I know its technically a new relationship, but nigga, you gave me a key and laid in the bed with me damn near every night!"

He pleaded with me to calm down and to understand that he hadn't meant to hurt me. I rolled my eyes and got up from the table. I felt betrayed. I was searching for my cardigan but he was already holding it. I snatched it out of his hand and damn near ripped it. "Please just give me five minutes to explain," he begged. When we locked eyes I saw fear in his. It wasn't enough to fully melt my rage, but it thawed it.

"I'll give you two minutes."

It took more than two minutes as he explained he had

a plan to hire a lawyer. The lawyer would negotiate the terms when he surrendered, that would make things easier. He wanted to build a life with me. "This is a weight that's keeping me from moving forward with us," he said. "I don't know how much time I will get but will you wait for me?"

I put my sweater down. "Yeah, I'll ride this out with you."

It felt like what I was supposed to do for my man and I imagined the process would be bearable, and overall worth it when we reconnected after his release.

We talked until the sun came up. I expressed my fears. He shared his. I shed tears. He held back his. We made plans for his mechanic business and talked about how we wanted to shape the rest of our relationship. Five months later he was gone.

My life was so different without Anthony. A few months before he turned himself in, I got a new job as a therapist in Dobbs Ferry, New York. The job kept me a lot busier than my old one. I was able to use my MSCJ to land that position because of psychology classes I took in grad school and the weekly clinical supervision my old company mandated. I was making almost double my previous salary and living alone in a family-owned town house I rented in Yonkers. Even though I was required to submit five different clinical reports each week, I made my own schedule so my workdays were flexible and allowed me to pour into my community by volunteering in church. I was teaching Bible classes on Tuesday evenings, assisting with a job readiness program on Wednesday evenings, and teaching the teen abstinence classes on Thursdays. Every other Saturday, I helped run a women's Bible study with a lady from my church. I needed to be surrounded by faith and prayer to help me during what had become my darkest nights.

Not seeing Anthony was incredibly hard. I spent the first few months crying myself to sleep. I was thankful to wake up knowing I had the church. In addition to the spiritual work and serving my community, I was happy to spend time around new people. When you don't want to be seen, new people are good covers. I spent far less time with my soul mates, Vonnie, Tonia, and Nellie, and though they never judged me, they did something worse—they saw me. I could pretend to be fine at church, but my soul mates could look at me and know that I wasn't. I was incredibly lonely and beyond exhausted. I thought about cutting back on some of my activities in the church. I met with one of the ministers from the church to talk about how tired I was and see who could take my place if I took a few things off my plate. Instead of brainstorming with me about ways to decrease some of my responsibilities, he made me feel guilty for being tired. "You shouldn't be getting physically tired if you are doing spiritual work," he said. I loved God and my community, so I continued to labor beyond my exhaustion. I did all this and still found time to support Anthony.

I never considered breaking up with Anthony or meeting somebody else. Instead, I locked away pieces of myself to help him feel free. I didn't date (or have sex with) anyone else for the entire three years he was gone so that I could demonstrate my loyalty to him. Even though my salary had doubled at my new job, I still had to babysit during after-school hours because I needed extra money. It cost me one dollar per minute to talk to Anthony on the phone. I once received a phone bill for $350 one month. The cost of my loyalty was high, and I was the only one paying. I later switched to having him call me on my cell phone. This new strategy required me to have my debit or credit card available whenever he called. When I answered the phone, an automated voice would say, "You have a collect call from…" The voice would pause and Anthony would state his name. "Press one to proceed." Proceeding meant putting my credit card number into the phone and giving the facility authorization to charge me for each minute we spoke. They limited each call to thirty minutes. As soon as the thirty minutes were up, the call would end without warning. We spoke two times a week. I drove six hours and spent weekends in hotels in Virginia to visit with him for an hour—the maximum time the facility allowed.

Since he had a child that predated our relationship, I did what I could to support her to help ease his stress. When I asked Anthony's sister Jamela how his daughter, Tiffany, was doing, Jamela told me things weren't going well with Tiffany's mother, Darlene. "Darlene was struggling with paying her electricity bill again," Jamela stated. I couldn't stomach the thought of his child's mother not being able to provide for their daughter. I responded without hesitating, "J, call Darlene and tell her I want to talk to her. Tell her Anthony gave me money to send them and I need her account number."

"Oh, I thought his shop closed down?"

"It did, J, but Darlene won't ask any questions. Nobody asks questions when you're sending them money."

"Girl, you really riding for ya man...that's why I love you."

"I love you too, J," I said before I climbed into bed and passed out.

I rarely expressed how emotionally draining this was for me. My role in our relationship was to protect him. As a ride-or-die chick, it was my duty to help him feel fully supported. One Sunday evening I was lying in bed considering calling it a night. It was around 8:30 p.m., but my body felt like it was midnight. My eyelids were heavy, and the TV was still on because I was too tired to search my bed for the remote and turn it off. I was drifting off, but I heard my cell phone ringing. It was downstairs. "Shit," I mumbled. I knew it was Anthony. This was our usual day and time to talk. I considered ignoring it, but there's always a chance that he could need my help with something. I pulled myself out of bed, grabbed my credit card from the bag hanging on the back of my bedroom door, and rushed downstairs. I pressed in my card number and released a faint smile when I heard, "Peace, queen."

"Hey," I responded.

"Were you able to follow up with the lawyer about my reconsideration process?" he asked.

"I called him, but he hasn't responded yet," I replied as I stretched to wake myself up.

"Did you and J make the last payment?" he asked, almost pleading. "If y'all didn't finish paying him, this might be why he's not returning your call."

I took a deep breath, rubbed my temple. "I don't exactly have five K lying around. I already gave J five hundred dollars to put towards the initial two K, plus it's kinda hard keeping up with bills in two separate homes."

"Thanks again for paying that bill for Darlene. She lost her job," he said sheepishly. "I wish I was home. I wish my plan to keep my business open worked, I wi—"

"I wish for a lot of things, Anthony, and none of this was part of my plan." My words hung in the air. It was the first time I shared my frustration with him. The silence was thick. "Anthony, this is hard."

"Did you meet somebody else? Is that why it's hard all of a sudden?" he yelled. "I was preparing myself for when you left me."

"ALL OF A SUDDEN?" I screamed back. "First of all, you've been locked up for almost three years. What the HELL are you talking about all of a sudden? And I didn't say I was leaving. I was just trying to explain—"

"I'm sorry," he cut me off. "Nita, I don't wanna argue with you. I know this a lot, and I appreciate everything you're doing. I know I'm asking a lot, but I don't really have anybody else. I go months without speaking to anyone on the outside except for you. I go through so much in here. This shit is insane. Ain't nothing like being locked up with a bunch of people you don't really know. This is nothing like doing a bid in a prison in New York where I am actually from... at least I have a chance of knowing somebody. Instead, I'm back in Virginia without anyone." I listened to him vent for twenty-five minutes. He rarely lamented for this long, and I assumed he must have really needed it. Since we were venting, I decided to try one more time to open up about exactly how draining life was for me too.

"Anthony, you're not the only one that doesn't have anyone to talk to. I don't really share how I'm feeling with the people closest to me because they might not understand why I stay with you. Sometimes it's hard to explain it to them and I don't always have you to talk—" *Click.* The thirty minutes were up. I never tried to express my emotions to him again. I felt too guilty…like I was wasting our calls.

We stayed together a year after he was released. When he came home, naturally I was thrilled, but within the first couple of hours I knew something was different with us and him. His first night home, he cooked dinner at my place. He was about thirty pounds heavier, and it looked great on him. I sat in the dining room and stared into the kitchen and watched him cook for us. It was a familiar scene, but the people were clearly different. He looked out of place and unsure how free he could be in my new home. "Is it okay if I use this bag of salad?"

"Of course," I responded with confusion.

"A brother hasn't had fresh vegetables in a minute," he stated as he patted his now bulging stomach. I giggled. He forced a smile. That night we ate in silence. He felt like a polite stranger to me. Three years of no physical connection with a person is hard. Three years of being in a relationship with a person who isn't reciprocating the emotional labor you're dispensing is even harder. I still loved the version of him that I met three years ago...deep down I was hoping that person would resurface again.

After years of paying for calls, sending packages, and helping with lawyer fees, I expected him to fulfill his prison promise. "When I come home, it's my turn to take care of you, queen." He had a hard time finding a job with the new felony conviction. He moved in with me and I continued waiting for my turn. I continued to take care of us. My car was ours. My town house was ours. Groceries were ours. Everything was ours except for the rent—that was mine. Internally, I was struggling with walking away. It's hard to know when to walk away after you've given so much. I kept thinking there would be a return on my investment. I was still waiting for "him" to come home.

He was so different from before he was incarcerated. Now he was insanely quick-tempered, thoughtless, and even cruel at times. Arguments escalated quickly. He would become defensive when I complained about him not putting gas in "our car." We were completely at odds about what his transition back into the professional world should look like. He wanted time to rebuild his old business. He didn't want to look for a job anymore, nor did he even want to work for anyone. "I'm not like you, I'm smart enough to build my own business from scratch. I don't need to wait for some white man to give me a check."

There was always some version of that statement when I asked about his job search. "I guess sitting around and waiting for a Black woman's check is better." I was now as quick-tempered as him.

I couldn't sustain the relationship. Emotionally and mentally, it was too much. And playing build-a-brother was expensive. After ending the relationship, I was stuck with debt and damage. I had a payment plan to pay off credit card bills, but there was no arrangement possible that could restore what I'd really lost. You never get back the energy and time you pour into a lopsided relationship.

I chose to endure that relationship because I had internalized a patriarchal narrative that stipulated that my needs were secondary in a romantic relationship with a man. A lot of Black women are conditioned to show love by proving how much difficulty we can endure for our men. Or rather how much we would "ride for him" and call it support. I was taking trips to another state to support my man because he was locked up. Paying his baby momma's light bill. All 'cause I loved and supported my man. That's classic ride-or-die mentality, and it's not relegated to a specific class of people. I had a master's degree and a career while I was sitting in a dingy facility talking to my boo through plexiglass. Pretending the concept of a ride-or-die chick is something that only applies to "those" women is a mistake. It detracts from self-analysis and keeps you from interrogating your own actions and producing change. The ride-or-die chick is a class-neutral concept that's toxic for Black women. It presents as virtue under the guise of *The Help*. There is an expectation that because she is a "strong Black woman" that she will always show up through all types of hardship; she takes care of everyone, her man, their children, and the community. She holds down a job and assumes most of the responsibilities, while saving nothing for herself and seldom seeking much in return.

Deconstructing and rejecting the notion of a ride-or-die chick is about more than just criticizing a song—or even critiquing hip-hop. It's about identifying how this message is consistent and accepted in multiple aspects of the Black community. This is why it's able to grow so strong within hip-hop. We connect to the song and messaging because it's familiar. We've seen it modeled all our lives. Hip-hop didn't create the problem, but it's certainly amplifying a message that's harming Black women.

When Black women internalize these expectations, we push ourselves to become this mythical superwoman,

and it's killing us. Dr. Cheryl Giscombé, a noted social
and health psychologist and a psychiatric–mental health
nurse practitioner, researched health disparities in Black
women. Her data indicates that "health disparities in African American women, including adverse birth outcomes,
lupus, obesity, and untreated depression, can be explained
by stress and coping. The Strong Black Woman/Superman
role has been highlighted as a phenomenon influencing
African American women's experiences and reports of
stress." Her data reiterates that the prioritization of a care-
giver role that supersedes individual needs and self-care
is connected to emotional suppression and contributes
to declining physical health in women. The research also
shows that these behavior patterns are generational, noting that this was modeled by our foremothers. According
to her research, Black women are especially susceptible to
overperforming as a way of dispelling racist perceptions—
like being intellectually inferior. Thus we are more likely
to overperform and become "superwomen" at work, in our
homes, and in our communities.

The health ailments outlined in Dr. Giscombé's research
are often fatal. Research around the correlation between
depression and health indicates that untreated depression
can, according to the blog *AFMindHack*, "cause blood ves-
sels to constrict, raising the risk of cardiovascular disease."

Data as recent as 2018 demonstrate that about 50 percent of Black American women have "some form of cardiovascular disease." This is higher than any other race of American women reported in the study. Studies also show people with undiagnosed depression are at a higher risk for suicide. This data coincides with the term "weathering," coined by Arline Geronimus, a public health researcher and professor at the University of Michigan's Population Studies Center. Geronimus's data stipulates that people of color are subjected to racism our entire lives. The stress of racism impacts our immune system and makes us more vulnerable to illness. The culmination of both bodies of research stipulates that Black women's health is compromised because of racism and internalized expectations to be a superwoman—which is tantamount to the concept of a ride or die.

Black men and Black women both experience racism in the United States. There is no prize for the person who gets harmed the most by racism. Yet, it is necessary to note that Black women are not only harmed by the physical ways that racism destroys our bodies, but we are *also* at risk of greater harm because we internalize and perpetuate the expectation that we should be everything to everyone, despite what it costs us. That means racism inflicted upon us by the United States is already deteriorating our health.

Black men contribute to this harm when they perpetuate the notion that Black women are their ride-or-die chicks. Black men may not shout from the rooftops the exact words "I want a ride-or-die chick," but when they have an expectation that Black women should continue to demonstrate our love and loyalty through unreciprocated labor, they become dangerous to us. The specific Black men who operate in this fashion are contributing to our deaths, and Black women who perpetuate it are aiding them.

Our community's survival is contingent upon us consistently organizing together to fight against racism. Moreover, Black women cannot continue to fight with Black men about sexism while contending with racism and simultaneously maintaining the emotional capacity to lift our communities. It will break us and our communities will shatter. The health of Black communities in the United States requires an all-hands-on-deck approach. This is a fight that needs us all.

Deconstructing and abolishing the concept of a ride-or-die chick is about more than my personal feelings around imbalanced relationships. It's about the overall harm it causes to generations of Black women and our communities. It's about loving and protecting Black women by eliminating what isn't working. Love doesn't negate accountability. Both Black men and Black women have to take accountability and reject the notion of a ride-or-die chick. We tell the white folks that admitting that racism exists isn't enough—we require them to be anti-racist. The same holds true for abolishing the notion of a ride or die. Being anti–ride or die is the standard. This means going beyond just acknowledging that it's toxic for Black women, but also committing to actions that will help eliminate it. The sustainability of our communities and an entire generation of young Black girls is depending on us to stop sampling and remixing this same song.

2

THE CORNERS

The problem that we endure is one of constant erasure.

—Treva B. Lindsey

There aren't many safe spaces for Black women and girls in the United States. Many spaces that offer a level of safety and comfort to Black boys and men offer far less of it to us. This is especially true of the corners in our own community. Whether you live in the Midwest or Brooklyn, there exists a universal experience for Black women on the corners in our hoods. The street corners for many Black men are where they found brotherhood, manhood, or safety, and it's evident in hip-hop songs and videos like "The Corner," a stand-out track on Common's album *Be,* where that is celebrated. But for Black women and our bodies, we have a complicated relationship and experience with those corners that has been invisible in our music and often ignored within our community. Songs like "The Corner" don't acknowledge the trauma and violence that Black women and girls endure on these corners. The juxtaposition of the experiences of Black women and men on these corners is symbolic of a larger community weak spot.

I love Common as an artist. Common is one of the

most conscious rappers in the industry, and he loves Black women. However, that doesn't negate the fact that his song, which captures the experiences of a lot of Black men with nuance and care, could have been more powerful if it included a candid look at what Black women experience on corners. Especially considering the sexual violence, antagonism, and assault Black women face on these corners, which remain largely unaddressed in our own communities.

It's easy to consider the erasure of our perspective from "The Corner" as just another artist making a song to simply celebrate a space that's culturally relevant to our men, without noting why including Black women in this narrative is important. That would be fine if the space in question was their "sacred" barber shop and not an unavoidable element in our community where walking by just to go home can mean being chased and assaulted by the very men who should be protecting you.

Black women need to make known the inner and emotional toll that we face. We have been constantly called out for our supposed tough exterior shell and given labels like "angry Black woman." However, for some Black women, this tough exterior shell was developed as a coping mechanism at a young age when we had to learn how to escape sexual advances from grown men while walking through our own neighborhoods.

The corners are a complex space in our community; in many cases, it's the origin for unaddressed trauma in both Black women and men. There has been awareness in our music about the harm to Black men—hunted by the police, profiled, wrongfully arrested, and more. But it's on these same corners that Black men have often hunted us and inflicted harm on Black girls and women. The corners are a space where police can snatch a brother's freedom and inflict pain on their bodies and force a massive community outcry. It's also the space where police have inflicted sexual violence against poor Black women and girls without impunity. Within our community, and by extension in hip-hop, these dualities are not unpacked enough. To unpack them, we have to tell a fuller story about those corners, a story that centers on the mute experiences of Black girls and women. We have to reflect on how this later impacts our love lives as women and the tropes we contend with, and even how we learn to compartmentalize sexual violence.

Common was not the only rapper to use a video and song to paint a picture of the corners that could've been more powerful if the lens was broadened. Jay-Z, one of hip-hop's best storytellers, illustrated this in his video for "Where I'm

From" and walked us through the blocks of pre-gentrified Brooklyn in "Hard Knock Life." From the corners of Chicago to the blocks in Brooklyn, the images all reflect dice games, crowds of men in front of a store, shit-talking, laughing and the police always present. There is no shortage of videos capturing the universal experiences of Black men on these corners. With few exceptions, the same can never be said of the experiences of Black girls and women.

In the video for "The Corner," a group of young girls are dismissed from school and walk toward the corner. The scene fades and the viewer never sees what happens to those girls. This is exactly what our missing narrative feels like in hip-hop—we know Black women and girls are present on those corners, but our stories are rarely fully explored. But if they were fully explored, listeners would understand that for a lot of Black girls, the first place they encountered sexual violence is from the older men in the neighborhood. It's the place where men publicly expressed an interest in their bodies. If these stories were ever fully told, listeners and viewers would learn that these corners are also a place where too many Black girls get used to this treatment, and it was not by choice but because of consistency.

It started for me when I was maybe twelve years old, but it could have been before then. According to the dudes on the corner, I was "stacked like a grown woman." Mentally, I was far from a grown woman; I still played with dolls at home. At the time, the most exciting aspect of life was my newly acquired freedom to walk unaccompanied to visit my cousins Tonia and Vonnie, to do things like roller-skate up and down the block, or to go see my girlfriend Mika so she could flat-iron my hair. My cousins and girlfriend lived in the same hood, so I would pass the same corner. I took the same route that was always interrupted by the same group of guys. There was never just one of them there. They rolled in droves. Some days, they'd scream things that they would do to my twelve-year-old body. I learned to walk faster. I would lower my head to make myself invisible. It didn't matter if I crossed the street away from where they stood or walked directly by them, they would make sure I heard them. I tried to shrink myself and cover my body, or wear things that were less revealing, but that didn't work. Soon I'd just walk by as if I didn't hear them. As a preteen, I learned that sexual harassment from grown men went by quicker if I pretended it wasn't happening.

Most days I wasn't afraid of them, I was embarrassed. I didn't become afraid until I knew they intended to make good on some of the promises they screamed. One day, the loudest man of the bunch interrupted his trash-talking with his friends and approached me. He knew my name, knew exactly where I was coming from, and even mentioned my older brother. "What's up lil Rome, you coming from Mika's house today?" I glanced up at him slowly. He was a large man, six foot three and stocky, eclipsing my five-foot-six, twelve-year-old self. He was handsome, with dark chocolate skin and wavy hair that I'm sure did him well in the '80s. He was in his late twenties and seemed to be popular with the other guys. A small part of me was flattered by the attention when he approached me, but I was still uncomfortable. He was "old." I was confused about why he would even look at me, much less approach me, especially since he knew my brother. I was annoyed at myself for not crossing the street fast enough and hoped he'd leave me alone. The look in his eyes hinted that he wouldn't. When he grabbed my ass, it confirmed that.

I had on my favorite sneakers—a pair of green 5411s—and sped off as quickly as I could. To my surprise, he ran after me. My heart skipped. Touching me was alarming, but *chasing* me was terrifying. I tried to dodge him by darting into the corner store where I usually purchased my "nowlater" candies. I ran inside and just stood there catching my breath for a few seconds.

"You have to buy something or leave," the man behind the counter yelled.

"I'm still looking," I said.

I walked down an aisle of potato chips, glancing over my shoulder to see if he came in the store behind me. He didn't. He stood outside looking at me through the front door. I walked to the back of the store and pretended to read labels of dog food. Despite not being a smoker I asked the cashier, "How much two 'loosies' cost?" I knew the cashier wouldn't sell me the cigarettes, but I figured I could haggle with him for a few minutes.

"What are you buying?" the cashier asked in the frustrated tone he usually reserved for customers he suspected of stealing.

I wanted to scream, "I'm not stealing, I need help," but I knew it wouldn't matter to him. I knew he was about to kick me out, but I managed to stand in the store for about another ten minutes. Just when I was about to leave, I heard the sound of the police outside the store. I looked and saw a verbal exchange between a cop and the man who'd chased me. A crowd formed around them. The cop said something to the man. The man put his head down. There was a scuffle. I heard an older woman yell, "Get ya hands off that boy, he just standing there about to go in the store, and you drove up and messed with him for nothing."

When the crowd thinned out, I saw the man being placed in the back of the police car. An older Black couple walked into the store. "Same cop always driving by, fucking with them same boys every day. Chasing them off the block. Putting their hands on them like it's nothing," the younger Black woman said.

"Always been like that, sister," the older Black man said.

The song describes the corners as *our magic, our music, our politics*. This is not the case for Black women and girls. For us, it's a space where girls as young as twelve can experience sexual harassment and sexual violence and never mention it to anyone. I never told anyone the guys harassed me almost every day—not my mom or older brothers. Part of me thought it was my fault. I felt like I was doing something wrong to be harassed like that. I must have worn the wrong pants to make him grab my butt. Part of me was flattered by it—I thought I must be cute, and this is what men did when they thought you were pretty.

At twelve years old, I was bigger than most of the other kids, so I got more attention from twenty-year-old guys than I did from other preteen boys. Most of the time it made me wish I was invisible, except for when I thought the guy was attractive. In those cases, I would feel conflicted. I knew street harassment was gross and inappropriate, yet even though I lowered my head and walked faster, I would always find a way to work it into a conversation with my friend Mika whenever we were alone at school.

In terms of outward appearances, Mika and I were

polar opposites. She was very slender, about five foot five, with a body that was far less developed than mine. Our bodies may have been different, but when we sat in our middle school lunchroom and exchanged stories about the men on the corner, our accounts were almost identical. "Girl, you know Terry was outside trying to get with me again?!" I would divulge to my friend, hoping my nonchalant tone was believable.

"Ewww, isn't he like twenty or something? That's gross. His older cousin Mark is always trying to get with me every time I see him around my bus stop," Mika would say, rolling her eyes.

Secretly we both felt good that an older guy could "like" us.

We had no language for what was happening, and therefore couldn't understand our conflicted emotions. It was merely something that happened to all the girls in our community, especially the well-developed ones like me or the cute ones like Mika—at least that's what we thought. We normalized it. Insecure preteen girls are like catnip to predators like Terry and Mark. I did not understand that he was preying on me. Predators are calculating and know exactly how to pace themselves. According to research conducted by Dr. Georgia M. Winters, sexual offenders seek potential victims with "perceived vulnerabilities that would allow the child to be more easily isolated from others, such as low self-esteem, low confidence, insecurity, neediness, or naivety." There is a large body of quantitative data to substantiate this, but talk to the Black women who crossed those corners, and they will provide you with enough qualitative data to rival most published studies. Unfortunately, we became experts in the field long before we developed the language and the ability to deconstruct it. For some of us, this happened before we were even out of our training bras. This is why hip-hop, out of all genres, owes it to us to present this perspective. Hip-hop was born out of a need to become a microphone for voices muted by white America. When hip-hop ignores and erases the voices of our community unless they belong to straight cis Black men, it operates like the same oppressive system it was created to contend with.

Listening to "The Corner" now as a grown woman with a daughter feels different. When the song plays, I experience the lyrics through the eyes of a young girl; I'm walking beside Common and looking around through the eyes of my twelve-year-old self. When Common says, *walking to the store for the rose, talking straightforward to hoes,* I mentally walked past that corner and remembered what it felt like to be the "hoe" men talked "straightforward" to. As I "walked" that corner with Common, I didn't have the empathy he shared for the men. He saw brothers who used drugs to *cope with the lows* and *niggas rolling in droves* because they had *nowhere to go*. In my mind, they were part of the large groups of older men with nowhere to go who violated and terrified me.

Common identifies the police as a source of terror on the corner, *the beasts roam the street, the police is Greek-like*. I could easily recall the countless times the police roamed our community. Even if you don't have personal childhood memories of the police in your neighborhood, there is no shortage of imagery in hip-hop depicting cops targeting Black men. In the Notorious B.I.G.'s "Juicy" video, we also see police pulling up to the corner and snatching Black men away from the community. There is no follow-up scene in "Juicy" letting the viewer know if they were incarcerated or killed. Either are likely outcomes. From the days of KRS-One's "Sound of Da Police" to the images from Tupac's "Trapped" video, the depictions of Black men being chased off the corner by the police constantly remind us they are hunted. Those types of visuals help our community empathize with our men around police violence. Conversely, there is a noticeable absence of similar imagery and lyrics that could produce more sympathy for Black women and girls.

Black women and girls are often left out of these

visualizations, but we are not shielded from police violence. For instance, in 2015, former police Officer Daniel
Holtzclaw was convicted of multiple counts of rape. The
investigations revealed he used his authority as an officer
to target Black women from low-income communities. He
would arrest them and give them the option of performing
sexual acts on him or go to jail. Holtzclaw's survivors later
indicated they never told anyone about the abuse because
they didn't think anyone would believe them. Holtzclaw
was not "one bad apple," he was the fruit of a corrupt
tree. In a report issued by the University of Florida's law
school entitled "The Violent State: Black Women's Invisible
Struggle Against Police Violence," the findings show that
rape against Black women by the police is severely "under-
reported, under-investigated and under-prosecuted." For
Black girls and women, the "beast" Common referenced
on these corners are both the predatory men "rolling in
droves" *and* the police roaming the street all "Greek-like."
Failing to use imagery and storytelling to amplify this message is another way hip-hop fails Black women and girls.
It's dangerous to perpetuate a narrative that police violence
is only a problem for Black men, when reports tell a different story. Common and every other artist with videos
and songs with this incomplete picture of those corners are
not the cause of the sexual violence police inflict on Black

women and girls. They are not responsible for rapes and police violence. However, artists like Common should be pushed to consider the impact their art could make if they included violence against Black women in their imagery and storytelling, because that would be a fuller, honest portrayal, and it's the truth.

Rappers who lack the range and skill set to tell a fuller story should use their platforms and power to uplift more Black female rappers who do.

The lives of Black women and girls on these corners aren't explored enough, and the lasting impact of these experiences deserves further examination. Queen Latifah touches the surface in the "U.N.I.T.Y." video. In the video, Latifah walks down the street and passes a crowd of men. One of the men grabs her ass and doesn't deny it when she calls him out on it. Latifah, more fearless than some of us, punches him in his face. But for every Latifah, there are dozens of Shanitas who didn't fight back. Regardless of the responses, many of us are still contending with the ramifications of the corner.

The corners were a double-edged sword; the more powerless we felt against the violence, the more we relied on coping mechanisms that we could control. As a young girl, I would try to focus my attention on anything except my surroundings. On my best days I could drown out the sounds of the men screaming about my body, but my friend Mika would do a lot more. In retaliation, Mika would swat away the hands of the older men grabbing at her body and scream, "FUCK YOU!" as she walked by.

"Girl, you aren't scared?" I would ask her whenever I saw her do that.

"Of course I am, but I can't let them see it. Fix your face, get tougher, and stop looking so timid, and they won't try to get with you so often." Mika was generous with tips about how to survive the corner. As we got older, she perfected an ability to scowl and appear tougher than she was, and I became a master at growing emotionally harder when faced with things that threatened my sense of peace and safety. I would emotionally retreat when I was afraid or hurt as a mitigation strategy. As an adult, when the pain of a failing relationship would prove to be too much, I would go into my emotional shell rather than face it. When in that mode, I would scowl, become easily agitated, closed off, and less responsive to emotional connections from anyone. My best friend, Yenny, said when I'm in this mode, neither loving words nor verbal attacks are able to impact me. They both roll off my back. She calls this my "rock mode," but I know the rest of the world sees only one thing: an "angry Black woman." The trope of the angry Black woman haunts too many Black women who survived those corners. We are painted as needlessly hostile, aggressive, overbearing, and even unlovable. Sometimes even our own men won't allow us to escape this stereotype. We get comments all the time from them on it: "I love our sisters, but y'all are just too hard." Phrases like this are uttered as a "joke" by brothers. "Damn, sis, just smile. You don't have to be so angry *all* the time." Total strangers will scream this when Black women walk by. The stereotype has been perpetuated in pop culture, TV, and films for several decades. It's an inescapable, harmful trope that results in people dismissing our rightful indignation and frustration, instead of fairly addressing the source of it. Some of us *are* angry Black women because we are sick of being erased, assaulted, unheard, and unprotected. Some of us are *not* angry Black women—we are just hiding behind a shell from a world of pain that oftentimes developed right in our community.

For many of us, the corners are the first place we developed a skewed understanding of abuse. It's where we learned to cope with our experiences by creating a litmus test for abuse that measures everything against the most extreme circumstances. This makes us more susceptible to domestic partner violence. When we reflect on the ways we were assaulted, taunted, terrified, or molested, we don't always label what we experienced as sexual violence because it wasn't rape. We measure our experiences against the more violent forms of sexual violations and decide that ours wasn't "that bad." When we get into the practice of not labeling and identifying abuse unless it's "extreme," we are more likely to stay in romantic relationships that are riddled with violence. I stayed in a relationship long past its expiration date because I didn't see an ex-lover's behavior as abusive, even though when he got angry at me, he would kick the screen of one of my plasma TVs until it shattered into pieces. When he didn't have the energy to kick one of my TVs, he would pour buckets of water on it to ruin it beyond repair. He wasn't physically kicking me, so I didn't see it as domestic abuse. When he would scream and curse at me so loudly that my neighbor once called me in tears because she was afraid for my life, I only felt ashamed because folks "knew my business," not fear that I was in a violent situation. I know women who had their face cut and walked around with permanent scars from lovers they never left. That was my litmus test for domestic violence, so according to that skewed method, I wasn't a victim of domestic violence. According to reports issued by the DOJ's Office of Justice Programs, this is common. The data shows that people who repeatedly experience early acts of sexual assault often struggle with recognizing different forms of inter-partner violence.

A skewed perception of violence is one of the more extreme ways the ramifications of these corner experiences are still present in our lives as grown women. They also appear in subtle ways that we simply characterize as part of our dating preferences. I was never shy about my attraction to really smart men with "two tablespoons of hood in them." I wanted my men well-read and aggressive—particularly in the way he pursued me. Yes, clearly communicating romantic interest is attractive, and anyone old enough to still call Sean Combs "Puffy" probably wants to avoid a "complicated" relationship status and is seeking something serious. But in order for me to even recognize romantic interest, I needed in-your-face, constant verbal affirmations about how dope I am, and just a tad of possessiveness for good measure. I learned this on those corners. Relationships that went from zero to one hundred in just a few months felt safest to me. Anything less than that left me questioning if he was genuinely interested. I wasn't the cliché that grew bored with "nice men." I just wasn't sure how to recognize them. If he wasn't trying to move at lightning speed, I thought he was more interested in a platonic friendship, so I would mentally place him in that infamous "friend zone." A struggle with identifying nonaggressive forms of affection is not uncommon in people who experienced repeated acts of sexual aggression as adolescents. Findings from the National Institutes of Health indicate that early acts of sexual aggression and violence can impact how we perceive and accept affection in adulthood. Some people struggle with completely forming emotional attachments, while others face challenges with understanding and defining healthy boundaries and connections. For women whose first experiences with opposite-sex attraction was convoluted by sexually aggressive predators that nobody ever labeled as such, issues around boundaries and affection blur together, and we begin to recognize romantic partnerships through a toxic lens. Connecting the dots between our current behaviors and past experiences can be a lifelong journey, and being honest about the origin is a solid start.

Whether the erasure of our experiences on these corners is an oversight or intentional almost doesn't matter because the impact feels the same. It's fitting that the hook on "The Corner" is *I wish I could give you this feeling.* I don't want Black men to feel erased in order for us to be heard. I don't want them to switch places with us. I want them instead to join us in the fight to protect Black women and girls from sexual violence. This means holding themselves and their friends accountable. Which means the brothers who see or even hear about their friends sexually violating Black girls and women have to speak up in our defense—at the very least.

I also want Black women who buried the trauma they faced on those corners to feel safe enough to unpack it so we can connect the experience to our current actions and begin to work through it and reimagine love and intimacy outside the scope of a toxic lens. I want Black women to feel affirmed and understand that sexual harassment and assault and domestic violence perpetrated against you at the hands of predatory men is not our fault. I want the hip-hop community as a whole to feel a greater responsibility to Black women and as a result center complex narratives about issues that harm us.

3

THAT THING YOU DO

If I didn't define myself for myself, I would be crunched into other people's fantasies for me and eaten alive.

—Audre Lorde

Black women win when we operate on our own terms, and not by the standards for our womanhood designed by and for men. It took me a long time to figure out this was "the thing" I was doing. In 1998, I was in my second year of college and away from everything and everyone I loved for the first time. When my family dropped me off on campus during my freshman year, my mom didn't cry. Instead, she said, "I know how you were raised. I know what seeds are inside of you. You will be fine or you will figure it out. You're going to learn a lot about yourself." My mom was right. In college, I learned a lot about the seeds that were inside me, but it turns out not everything planted grows the way we intend it to. I didn't know this until I was older and had to look at what was produced.

Growing up my oldest brother, Kia, was my first "Black studies professor" who schooled me on all the songs, albums, and artists that were unapologetically pro-Black. I didn't realize this at the time but my "syllabus" was composed of content that centered on Black American lives and experiences that was exclusively shaped by and told through Black men. He introduced me to teachings of Malcolm X, the writer Donald Goines, and Nas. The music he solidified as "authentic" hip-hop were songs like "Black Girl Lost."

In "Black Girl Lost," Nas uses mini vignettes to show us the different ways a Black girl becomes lost and what it means to be lost. According to Nas, a lost Black girl starts out as a *young, wild, beautiful love child* and as the song stipulates, ends up becoming someone who should be "ashamed" of herself. On her road to Black womanhood she experiences things like showing up for a job interview but realizing that the boss is only interested in having sex with her. A lost Black girl is also personally responsible when a guy she was intimate with later hurts her. Or as Nas states, *Niggas thirst you, you just let them hurt you and leave / What up ma, frontin' like you naive.*

"Black Girl Lost" is a nod to a Donald Goines novel with the same title. Goines shared a graphic tale of what constitutes a lost Black girl and how it happens. The hood classic is full of stories of her rape and other forms of violence. I never questioned what it meant that stories about young Black girls received titles like "lost" instead of labels that elicited less judgment like "endangered."

In the early '90s, our community called Black boys and men endangered as a way to underscore their need for protection against racism and various forms of violence. I accepted this as standard and never considered how years of exclusively learning about Black womanhood, culture, social justice, and history only filtered through the lens of Black men would shape how I defined myself and other Black women in rigid and judgmental terms.

Even worse, I capitulated to and reinforced a version of Black womanhood that didn't leave room for labels like endangered that evoked community protection and empathy. Instead, I labeled the girls I saw as "lost" too.

When Black women did things like "let herself get used by a man," were "too loud," or shook her ass in the clubs "too much," I labeled them lost. In my world, the lost girls had sex without being monogamous, or committed the worst act of self-hate on the planet: refusing to wear her hair natural.

Lost meant they were not even close to being where or who they "should" be. Even when I didn't verbally call them lost I mentally decided they were less than me and worthy of less protection and respect. It took me a long time to realize that I needed to unlearn the harmful narratives that were causing me to operate by a narrow standard of Black womanhood.

During this time Lauryn Hill exploded on the music scene as a solo artist, and I loved her immediately. The world had been waiting to see if the female MC who'd captivated hip-hop heads in the three-person group The Fugees could hold her own. She felt familiar and relatable. Not only did she hold her own, but she changed the game. Lauryn made history. Her first album, *The Miseducation of Lauryn Hill,* sold more than ten million copies. She was the first hip-hop artist to win the coveted Grammy for Album of the Year and was the first woman to take home five Grammy Awards in one night. The album comprises sixteen tracks, and each song—from the intro to the last—felt personal and intimate. Lauryn Hill was like our priestess; the song "Doo Wop" on the album uplifted and empowered us Black women, or at least the only version of Black womanhood I considered acceptable. At the time I thought "Doo Wop" spoke realness and wisdom into us with lyrics like, *when you give it up so easy you ain't even foolin' him / if you did it then, then you'd probably fuck again.*

The first time I heard "Ex-Factor" I was sitting in a truck with one of my fraternity brothers from South Carolina State University. He wasn't my boyfriend but we liked each other a lot and took our time dating. Jamal was about six foot four and thick, had light skin and chunky black curls that he kept cut in a mini 'fro. His black wire-framed glasses made his high cheekbones appear even more pronounced. I was typically attracted to brothers who looked more like Mekhi Phifer than those who looked like Al B. Sure, but Jamal was an exception. He was wiser and more mature than me. I was a sophomore who didn't know how to drive and was still living on campus trying to figure out what I wanted to do with my life. Jamal would drive his silver Pathfinder from his house in Columbia to come visit me in Sumter. It was a two-hour drive round trip, but he would always find the time to visit almost every weekend. He was a second-year law student with an internship at a prestigious firm that was sure to aid his well-crafted plan to segue into corporate law. His clear focus and maturity made me feel like I needed to get my shit together. Whenever we spoke, I usually did more listening than talking. I was intimidated by him as much as I admired his assurance and intellect.

One warm fall night Jamal came to visit me, and we parked his truck in a park near my campus to listen to the song "Ex-Factor." I sat in the spacious passenger seat comfortably staring at him as he appeared to be watching a private concert in his head. He faced the front window with his eyes closed, singing the line *Tell me who I have to be / To get some reciprocity.* It would be decades before I fully considered what a relationship with reciprocity entailed, but on that night I had no clue what Lauryn meant. "Man, I swear I don't even think most folks even heard that word until Lauryn said it," I said to him. He laughed and I giggled to hide my embarrassment. He didn't know it, but I was "most folks."

"See, no one loves you more than me / And no one ever will," he sang/spoke the verse back to me. I could hear the admiration for her in his voice and the connection he was experiencing. He shook his head and pressed pause on the CD player. "Lauryn is a beautiful queen," he said into the silence. "She is the type of woman you marry. She's one of those smart and soulful Black women, you know." I nodded. He continued, "Not like some of them other female rappers out here just talking about who they want to have sex with and running around naked and shit. I can't even imagine being like those sell-out brothers and as soon as they get a good job they marry the first white girl they find. Not marrying a sister isn't even an option for me. I just need them all to be more like you and Lauryn and not like you know…them other chicks." He smiled and tenderly stroked my natural 'fro. I had my favorite blue-and-white scarf wrapped around it. It was 1998 and the "other" Black women that he shook his head in disgust at were MCs like Lil' Kim and Foxy Brown. Neither Kim nor Foxy had a problem telling you how they liked to cum and Jamal didn't like that. For him, this didn't make them queens, and hence worthy to be married. The song continued to

play and I leaned in to both the talented and beautiful artistic expressions from Lauryn and the familiar feeling of a man I valued. I was convinced I needed to replicate the queen in order to get his respect, which I wanted so much.

Being called a queen always felt like both a compliment and a call to perform a very specific type of Black womanhood with a goal of the "ultimate" societal prize: being called a wife. Whether wife, wifey, or queen—she's got the respect of Black men. Being a wife is a beautiful thing and queens are regal and powerful. This only becomes a problem when we use labels like queen as a way to reinforce the false notion that only Black women who rock natural hair, know all the trendy social justice buzzwords, are sexually conservative, modestly dressed, and more demure, deserve more respect than other sisters. Oftentimes when men use these titles exclusively for women who fit that description, it implies that the sisters who fall outside that narrow concept of Black womanhood are "lost," less worthy of respect, and aren't "suitable" for marriage or protection.

My definition of Black womanhood—the queen, under the gaze, standards, and perception of Black men—formed at an early age. As a kid, I always gravitated toward the books and music my fourteen-year-old brother, Kia, enjoyed. Even at such a young age, Kia was my father figure and hero. Our biological dad lived in the projects across town with another family. Geographically he was about three miles from us but emotionally speaking there was no GPS that could have directed me to him. "We are the family God gave him, but that's the family he chose. Those are his children." That's the way Kia explained it to me as a child when our dad didn't buy us anything one Christmas because he spent all his money on his girlfriend's children. Kia's unfiltered words were meant to heal my pain but they just further bruised an already broken heart. I always tried to pretend that when our dad left he didn't take a piece of me with him. I was a toddler so that made the lie easier because you can't miss what you never had. That was the go-to attitude of every person I knew without a father in their life. Deep down his absence was always a presence in my life.

By the time I was eleven, my mom moved in with a guy named Tony who would later become my stepdad and a great help to my mom. On Christmas, my more expensive gifts would typically come from him. "Thank you, Tony," I'd shout about my new toy or leather coat. He was Tony. Not Dad, or Pop. We were on a first-name basis because that was the nature of our relationship and neither of us ever questioned it. I wasn't his daughter and we knew that. I wasn't my father's daughter either—and I knew that too. I also knew what a dad was supposed to be.

I had a front row seat to the way he loved his biological

son TJ. Still, Tony would deliberately make sure his son knew he was separate from my two brothers and me. Tony would do things like buy family-sized snacks for TJ to keep in his dresser rather than place them in the kitchen for us to share. I told myself that Tony wasn't trying to be mean to me or my brothers, these were just the types of things dads do to show their own children they are special. I would pretend to believe the lie. The truth was that my biological dad was prioritizing somebody else's daughter while I lived with a man who was intentional about showing his son we were second-class citizens.

"Y'all was never supposed to move in with us," TJ would say. "My dad bought this town house for just me and him...then your mom moved in with her three kids."

It was believable because the six of us lived in a two-bedroom town house. The three boys shared a spacious room and I slept in the living room. Before we invaded TJ's home, my brothers and I lived in Mulford Garden Housing Projects in Yonkers. It's where I first learned that mice become loudest at night and the only place to ease my fear of them was at the foot of Kia's bed. As soon as I heard mice scurry around our tiny two-bedroom apartment I would leap from my bed to Kia's. That's the only way I could fall back asleep. Even his sleeping presence brought me comfort.

I was a priority in Kia's world. When he would travel to 125th Street to buy books from tables that sold incense, ankhs, and shea butter, he would always return with an extra book for me and nobody else. I never heard of "Dr." Malachi York but according to Kia, his book is what I needed to have "my eyes open." Hell, I didn't know they were closed.

"When you read Dr. York you will understand why you don't need a perm in your hair," Kia would say. "You don't need to look like a blond-haired, blue-eyed Jesus. And make sure you never wear tight clothes. I know you're about to start seventh grade but don't be like those other girls. They just want to get attention from boys."

"So if Jesus didn't have blond hair and blue eyes why does he look like that in all the pictures at church?" I asked, genuinely confused.

"Slavery," he said.

As always, I walked away confused as hell. But to me, Kia was the smartest person in the world. If he said I should make sure to not be like those "other girls" then I needed to find a way to distinguish myself—whatever that meant. Kia said Dr. York was the truth. There was no Google in that time to tell me that Dr. York was suspected and later convicted of abusing fifty to seventy-five children, the mothers of whom were members of his "Nuwaubian Teachings." Even if there was, at fourteen Kia was my search engine.

Kia's opinions shaped what I considered meaningful and authentic. This has always been especially true of race analysis and hip-hop. I never needed "five mics" from *The Source* magazine to tell me an artist was dope—once I saw Kia listen to a song with his face twisted up like he was sucking lemons I knew it was a classic. Artists who rapped about Black consciousness and social injustices would always earn that look from him. Which meant it was only a matter of time before they became my favorite. When I went into his bedroom and saw a book with pages bent and the paperback cover cracked and tattered from constant use, it wouldn't be long before I discovered my own favorite pages to dog-ear in his book. While my peers were still paging through Sweet Valley High books by Francine Pascal, I was reading *Black Girl Lost* by Donald Goines—the story of a young Black girl with an absent father whose road to womanhood was riddled with sexual abuse and violence.

While at college, I never got into a serious relationship with Jamal. He became more focused on his law career, and I was still trying to become the queen he thought I should be. Naturally, my days of Dark and Lovely do-it-yourself relaxers in a box came to an end. Again, this was 1998, long before there were YouTube tutorials designed to spare newly natural sisters from the horrors of improperly caring for our unique curl patterns. I had a dried head of hair full of potential but void of style. Think Frederick Douglass, but with a headband. I thought it was cute in that way moms think their wrinkly newborn baby is adorable. It was mine and I loved it. Besides, I got a thrill out of walking around with my natural hair among Black girls who didn't. *They're not bold enough to rock their natural curl pattern like me,* I thought. They're lost.

The day I cut the last bit of the relaxer out of my hair, I sat in my small dorm room barely tolerating the Atlanta-based rap group OutKast that my roommate was blasting. Tamera was a native New Yorker who'd migrated to South Carolina as a teen. I looked at her newly acquired taste for Southern rap as a welcome-to-the-South gift many native New Yorkers tend to receive after relocating. I didn't see the beauty in Southern rap back then. I was New York hip-hop to my core. I tolerated this "flaw" in my roommate because she was dope. She was a smart, passionate, beautiful brown girl with full lips, a wide smile, and an almond-shaped head that seemed designed for her cute 'fro. When we first met, I kept a comfortable emotional distance. My natural inclination to be distrustful of strangers was the parting gift from New York I refused to unpack.

The distance between us started to fade as we spent more time together. Some days I stared at her in amazement for daring to transition from a cute little 'fro to short locs. She asked my friend Ashley and me to help loc her hair. We had no clue what we were doing. We parted her hair into medium-sized sections and used beeswax to twist her hair until it was as tight as it could go. I named the first one I twisted "Mahogany" and she promised to never cut it. It took us a few hours but when the three of us finished Tamera's hair, she became one of the first girls on our campus to have locs.

Although my school was one of the many Historically Black Colleges and Universities (HBCUs) in the United States, in 1998 a lot of the sisters on my tiny campus weren't exactly receptive to any form of hair worn naturally. And by "not receptive," I mean that at any given moment a woman with a long, bright-colored weave would frown at Tamera and ask why she "did that to herself" while pointing to her hair. The more they questioned her hair, the more I questioned their choices.

"Like, why can't these sisters love themselves enough to free their heads from that oppressive-looking weave in this merciless Southern heat?" I'd say to Tamera. "Blond weaves? Really? Come on, Black woman, you look ridiculous." I would roll my eyes, my judgment masked as defending my friend.

The other women's comments would usually be followed by a thinly veiled insult about something Tamera was wearing. If locs were enough to draw attention, the headwraps and long flowing skirts caused more than a few double takes when we walked through the congested student center. While Tamera's style stood in contrast to my bootcut jeans, fitted shirt, and heels, I resented the way she was received by women I labeled small-minded. I didn't have an accurate word for them, but I knew there was a "them." "Them" girls were different. "They couldn't even entertain the idea of loving themselves enough to be caught dead without blond weaves and tiny skirts," I would say to my girls anytime I saw one of them.

Tamera on the other hand had a different response. "Why do those girls bother you so much, Nita?" she asked me one day.

I looked at her in astonishment for asking me that. "Those birds with the long blond weaves who are looking at you like you're a mess for having locs? Or the ones with the tiny-ass skirts with their ass hanging out acting like you're the weirdo because your skirt is ankle length? By the way, everything about your look is giving me Erykah Badu and I love it, girl." Tamera had sewed a piece of her headwrap onto the hem of her denim skirt.

"Nita, if I had on a tiny skirt with this tank top instead of this long one, would I be a bird too?" she asked me, smiling. "By the way, calling those girls birds must be some leftover Yonkers residue, huh?" Tamera laughed the way she always did whenever I casually used old school New York slang. Her laugh faded but the question lingered.

I didn't pause to search for the answer, I paused because once again I was shocked at her question. "Of course not," I said. "You're nothing like those other girls...you know, look at them."

"So is it their hair or clothes that make them less than us—or birds, like you say?"

Tamera looked at me like she already knew the answer. Our walk from the cafeteria felt longer under the weight of her questions.

"It's all of it, girl, just ALL of it," I said. "First of all, Tina is a bird but she's not as bad as the rest of her crew. I had a few classes with her. She's smart, but damn, it seems like she forgets that when it comes to Jason. I heard her after class damn near crying to her soror about how Jason was a dick because he stopped answering her calls after they had sex. I wish we were actual friends so I could've told her that Jason was ignoring her because she had sex with him too quick. What did she expect?"

"Perhaps respect," Tamera spewed as she shifted her books around her arms. "Nita, I'm going to the room so I can drop these books off, plus you're getting on my nerves." From the looks of her, I didn't know what was getting harder for her to carry, the constitutional law textbooks or the burden of trying to remain composed.

"But you still love me. See you back in the room later," I said in between chuckles as I walked into the building to attend my African American history class. She laughed too but I could tell she meant every word.

Some moments in life come with a soundtrack so perfectly tailored for who you are that it feels scripted. Lauryn Hill's *Miseducation* was one of those soundtracks for me.

I was still ruminating on my professor's lecture on my way home from class. It had been on Charleston being the first destination of our enslaved ancestors. My college was less than two hours from Charleston, and it made me feel closer to my ancestors than ever. I was surrounded by the pieces of them that had been preserved—the Southern food and Gullah Geechee language. I was also reminded daily of what was stolen from us and how we had conformed to standards of beauty that we didn't create. My thoughts floated with me through campus as I took in the Black girls I'd labeled "birds," and when I walked into my room to the sound of Lauryn Hill's "Doo Wop" on the *Miseducation* album, everything in my being felt validated. Tamera was blasting it and Lauryn's words echoed off the walls and stopped me in my tracks. The music felt louder. The bass vibrated through the speakers, expanding our little dorm room into a concert hall.

I looked toward Tamera who was already searching my face to see if I liked it. I squinted and nodded like I was sucking on a lemon. Prior to that date I'd only heard "Ex-Factor" with Jamal, but this day we sat in my room and listened to the entire body of work. I thought it was perfect. Lauren's lyrics pulled no punches and it felt like she too had been thinking about conformity and beauty standards in the same way I had: *It's silly when girls sell their souls because it's in / Look at where you be in, hair weaves like Europeans / Fake nails done by Koreans.*

I gave a strong head nod, feeling every one of her lyrics deeply. At the time Lauryn rocked jet-black, beautiful, thick, free-form locs. She was a stark contrast to the other rappers who were topping the charts at the time, like the late DMX, OutKast, and Jay-Z. Yet here she was going toe-to-toe with the hip-hop heavyweights. She was a twenty-two-year-old Black woman and the most socially conscious and thoughtful lyricist in hip-hop I'd ever heard. She felt like my brother Kia: safe and brilliantly upholding the acceptable standard of Black womanhood.

I was too young to appreciate the Black girl magic of female pioneers like Queen Latifah and Monie Love, which made me love Lauryn even more. Rappers like Queen Latifah and Monie Love were intersectional feminists, although the phrase was not part of the mainstream lexicon in the late '80s. Both Monie and Latifah understood and rapped about the overlapping forms of oppression that made Black women's struggles distinct from our brothers. But though I knew their music, I didn't connect with them, at least not in the same way I did with Lauryn. Lauryn's lyrics mirrored my own thoughts and echoed many that Kia shared with me. Especially when it came to those "other" Black women who slept with men "too quickly." This sentiment was my gold standard—even more so since it was echoed by a conscious rap "god" like Nas in his song "Black Girl Lost." *Niggas thirst you, you just let em hurt you and leave / What up ma, fronting like you naive.*

There was always some version of this line passed on to me as a cautionary tale. Lauryn sounded exactly like Nas, which made the first verse in "Doo Wop" my favorite.

> It's been three weeks since you were looking for your
>   friend
> The one you let hit it and never called you again
> . . .
> Plus, when you give it up so easy you ain't even foolin'
>   him
> If you did it then, then you'd probably fuck again

Was Tamera hearing this? There were so many lyrics that confirmed who the "birds" were! *Showing off your ass 'cause you're thinking it's a trend.*

"Girl, yes," I said looking over at Tamera, waving my hand to the beat in praise. Couldn't Tamera see that "queens" like us were not birds? We were a different type of Black woman, the kind who was worthy of respect. Lauryn was making that clear. We stayed in our room listening to the full CD and I continued to fall in love with the details of Lauryn's music. I had always loved the question that she posed at the end of "Doo Wop": *How you gonna win when you ain't right within?*

My friends and I were part of Lauryn's tribe and winning. We were conscious Black women—we could quote Carter G. Woodson in our sleep, were committed to "fixing" the racist criminal justice system, preferred open mics over clubs, didn't sleep with men "too quickly," and had natural hair.

Plus the brothers called me queen. They constantly said I was nothing like those "other girls," and I considered it a supreme compliment. Being called a queen was their recognition of my Black girl magic. In 1998 we weren't using the phrase "Black girl magic" yet, but the essence of it was always clear and queen meant that Black men saw that in me, and it was invaluable. My self-worth was connected to being viewed by men as separate from those other girls, which was only a softer way of saying I'm better than those girls. Or at least that's how it registered to me.

I swam in Lauryn's words because she validated the piece of me that needed to be considered separate and unequal to other women. Being considered different from the other girls who had sex too quickly, wore straight hair and weaves, were loud, rocked tight clothes, and hung out in the clubs felt like I had the "right" version of Black womanhood that would equal success, love, male adoration, and respect. It felt like I was winning like Lauryn stated. It took me a long time to understand that if winning meant "conscious queens" were granted permission to use a skewed standard of Black womanhood defined by men to marginalize other sisters, then perhaps we needed to lose.

Conscious queens raised on a steady diet of New York hip-hop weren't the only sisters who thought this way. There were plenty of sisters born and bred all around the country, south or north of the Mason-Dixon Line who aimed to mirror this acceptable version of Black womanhood. My friend Vanessa had flawless skin the color of coffee diluted with just a dash of milk. Her eyes were large and cat-shaped with lashes so long they still called out to you beneath her glasses. She had a laugh that matched her magnetic personality and beauty. Magnetic wasn't the word Vanessa used to describe herself but that's who she was. She was full of witty jokes and captivating stories about her plans to take over corporate America. When we were in the presence of men she was attracted to, I noticed how her personality would shift. Suddenly the hilarious, outspoken, and bold Vanessa would appear introverted, timidly touching her face and laughing too hard at all their jokes. "I carry myself differently so men know I'm the type of woman they should marry," she told me one day when I called her out on this behavior. "I want them to know that I'm not the type of woman who they should just play around with."

It surprised me that it was even a concern of hers but also that she thought this was the way to win a man. She was one of the smartest and most fearless women on campus. She was the only one answering professors' questions while the rest of us slouched down in hiding. She had all the answers. I was secretly in awe of her from the first day we met in our economics class.

Economics was an hour-long class but it always felt like a full day. Time stands still when you're spending every second wishing the most intimidating professor on campus doesn't call on you for anything. This particular class felt safer because of Vanessa in the front row. Whenever Professor Jones explained a concept, he was met with blank stares and awkward silence. When the silence lingered too long we all knew he would grow frustrated and assign more homework to help us understand. Just as he was about to administer the assignment, Vanessa interjected and asked a question that would require him to talk until the class ended. One day I walked out of class and approached my savior. "Hey, have you taken a class with Professor Jones before? You seem like the only person who isn't afraid of him. Plus I heard you're the only student here who currently has an A in this class," I stated as we walked out of the building.

"The trick is to always complete the homework assignments. The questions for his tests come directly from the homework."

"Girl that only helps if you actually understand the homework," I said while holding up my newly returned assignment. Practically every question was marked wrong. "If I don't get my shit together in this class my 3.2 GPA is finished."

"Meet me in the library Tuesday at seven p.m. and I'll help you." We never said more than a few words to each other prior to this exchange so I was overwhelmed with her offer.

"Thank you," I said and began squeezing the life out of her. After that Vanessa and I grew from casual classmates to good friends who ended up sharing more in common than we thought.

"Southern women aren't like those…other girls," Vanessa quipped while we were sitting in the student center eating overpriced chicken fingers and watching the "Doo Wop" video. She was gazing at a group of girls sitting a few tables behind us. I followed her disgusted gaze and saw that it had landed on a table full of women from New York. I knew all four of them. Whenever there was a break in the semester we would coordinate travel arrangements together. Sometimes we would split the cost of gas to ride back together to New York for Christmas break. Other times we would synchronize our scheduled flights home so that we could help each other get to the airport from campus. Aside from that, and our shared experience of navigating Southern culture for the first time, our connection didn't travel into our social circles. If our main friends weren't available, we would walk to the café together and sometimes borrow textbooks from one another. But on this particular day my blood started to boil the moment I spotted the targets of Vanessa's disgust.

"I have secondhand embarrassment just watching them," Vanessa said.

I rolled my eyes because I knew this was another one of her "New York women are too hard to be marriage material" moments she liked to casually interject into our conversations around relationships. "Vanessa, girl, what are you talking about?"

"Nita, don't you hear those loud and rowdy women behind us? They sound like my dad and his friends—cursing all loud, talking at the top of their lungs. Only things missing are the cigars and beer. I don't know how they expect to attract a man by acting like one. They are too much."

"Laughing too loud. Being too excited. Having fun in public. Got it. I'm mentally adding this to Vanessa's list of things New York women do that are too hard."

Vanessa had a little mental box that Black women needed to neatly fit into in order to be considered marriage material. Unlike Jamal she never dished out titles like queen. Instead she used the label "marriage material" to indicate there is a version of Black womanhood we must perform to be chosen and respected by men. "Vanessa, you are a mess. Who are you to decide that they are too much of anything? At some point you have to ask yourself why you need to see them as 'not marriage material' and why the hell that matters so much anyway." I pushed my food away and sat in silence while I tried to figure out if I was more offended because I recognized pieces of myself in Vanessa or because I recognized pieces of myself in the group of women. Listening to Vanessa felt like I was looking in a mirror and I didn't like the reflection. It was easier to "break the glass" than it was to stare at the reflection, so I lashed out harder at Vanessa. "Everything about the South is slow—the fashion is years behind, the good music never makes it to these wack-ass radio stations, and the collective thinking about women is stuck in the fifties."

"Why are you getting offended, Nita? You aren't like those other loud, hard New York girls. Those girls," she said, gesturing flippantly with her hand, "are the ones Lauryn was talking about when she said, *'Don't be a hard rock when you really are a gem.'*" She chuckled. The speakers had Lauryn booming in the background. "By the way, can I borrow *Miseducation*? I can't find my copy anywhere. I'm starting to think your roommate took it."

"Vanessa, you know my roommate's name, stop being silly," I said. "Besides that's not my copy it's actually Tamera's." Vanessa and Tamera always bumped heads around every topic under the sun, but Tamera was less patient with Vanessa than she was with me. *Showing off your ass 'cause you're thinking it's a trend* was more than just Vanessa's favorite line in "Doo Wop"—it was her mantra. The way Vanessa spoke about other women irritated Tamera and she always let her know it.

"Vanessa, how much longer are you going to let your dad's warning of becoming 'loose and not marriage material' shape the decisions your grown ass makes?" Tamera asked this question every time Vanessa muttered anything about dressing like a wife if you wanted to be treated like a wife.

I was usually silent when they feuded. Typically I fit into Vanessa's little box and displayed the "right" type of womanhood. We both created boxes and labels for other sisters. The ones who slept around too quickly were setting themselves up to be manipulated by men. Women who cackled fully at things that made them laugh, who expressed themselves with hairstyles and colors that were out of the box, and yes, who loved men to a fault, those girls were lost. They were birds and we were queens. The ones who wore revealing clothes were lost. The sisters who weren't natural were birds. I was fine with the boxes and labels. Hell, I was cool with weaponizing Lauryn's words to take shots at other women. It was all good until Vanessa continuously used male-centered standards of womanhood against women like me—those who were from "up north" and acted too hard, which didn't make us marriage material according to her. It bothered me to listen to her put sisters in a box that I could also be stored in.

Sure, when I asked her about it, she said I was different,

but in those moments it felt like I was talking to a white friend who was insisting I'm not like those other Black girls. I didn't understand it at the time, but women like Vanessa and I were gladly spewing an oppressive version of Black womanhood that was laced with respectability politics. We were contributing to our collective and individual harm as Black women. Respectability politics presents a false sense of safety from the "isms" of the world—racism, sexism, classism. It is the driving force behind the notion that if Black people dress in our Sunday best, speak the King's English, and avoid doing anything that would perpetuate racist stereotypes, then racist white people will treat us better. It's a misguided attempt to remain safer from the perils of oppression. While our boys and men are told things like "pull your pants up and dress with dignity," Black women are told not to be too loud or aggressive when we speak. We're not supposed to dress or appear too sexy either. Don't wear your nails too long at work. Make sure your hair is straightened on job interviews with your edges laid.

These are things that we were told will help us appear neater and professional. It will make us better girlfriend or marriage material. This type of verbiage didn't start with Lauryn Hill's "Doo Wop." These words—and all the variants—are passed down in families like old recipes. It's rooted in the notion that there is something a Black woman can do, wear, or say that will make her less vulnerable to men who want to harm her and less susceptible to racist labeling. Our foremothers and fathers didn't donate this perspective to us out of naivete. They lived through decades of violence and sheer disregard for our well-being. Black elders know there have been little to no consequences for harming Black people in any capacity. In response to this they tried to find ways to help us "protect ourselves." For some of them, clinging to respectability politics was their effort at protecting themselves. Still, despite their intentions, conforming to respectability politics in any form will never save us—it only exhausts us. The truth is whether your hair is natural or relaxed, whether you have sex with a lot of dudes or no one at all, or are a hard rock or a gem, changing our behavior will not make racist white people suddenly diverge from the systems of oppression they designed against us.

The irony is that most Black men understand this. They know respectability politics has never saved Black men or women from mass incarceration, police violence, discriminatory lending practices, and any other weapons of mass destruction. Similarly, Black women's adherence to respectability politics will not cause men to divest from sexist power structures and dynamics that were established to benefit them. When we reinforce shallow and sexist standards of womanhood we hurt each other and completely miss the magic of who we truly are. Black women are multifaceted. We can be the ankh-wearing sister with a fresh twist-out on Thursday night, and spend Saturday nights at the club throwing our ass in a circle wearing our best straight-haired wig. If we choose to, we can show off our ass without giving a damn about a trend. We can do all this and still be worthy of respect, protection, and love. None of this makes us any less "royal." The process of decentering a male version of Black womanhood requires unlearning. Reframing our thinking around empowerment and liberation is a generational obligation in the Black community—as our history and identity were taken hostage by white supremacy—and we'll be undoing and unlearning oppressive ideals for a long time.

Lauryn Hill is a gifted sister who taught us what she could in *Miseducation*, but we must consciously commit to continuing that process. However, this does not always translate into immediate change. We have to give ourselves and other Black women freedom to fall during this process. This means withholding judgment and being softer with each other. Lauryn may feel differently now than she did when writing the song "Doo Wop." Yet even if she doesn't, the response remains the same: we have to give each other freedom; giving each other the freedom to make mistakes and unlearn centuries of conditioning will make us stronger as a community, and better able to express our individual ideas so we don't get trapped in boxes. It is the only way we will ever be right within. To paraphrase a beautifully complicated and wise Black woman, *How we gonna win when we ain't right within?*

4:44

You've got to learn to leave the table when love's no longer being served.

—Nina Simone

When Jay-Z released the album *4:44* there was an explosive, universal celebration of his maturity, vulnerability, and growth. A lot of hip-hop fans called the song "4:44" (of the album's same name) his most introspective work to date. The song itself was a remorseful, beautifully written open letter to the women he'd hurt throughout his life. He shared his regrets about womanizing and the way that fatherhood had transformed him. He told the world the birth of his daughter, Blue Ivy, helped him finally see the world the way she might see it one day.

Parenthood is in fact life-changing and often shifts our worldview. However, it's worth noting that at the time Jay-Z released this song in 2017 he was already the son of a Black mother, brother to a Black sister, and husband of a Black wife. He was also a forty-seven-year-old man who, according to his own songs, had had plenty of relationships with different women.

Still, when the song was released, I was the first in line to celebrate his growth. An artist of Jay's stature publicly apologizing to the women he hurt? It was love at first hook

for me. I wasted no time turning my group chats into a
Jay lovefest, calling the song an example of grown-man
rap. I wasn't alone in my celebration. From social media
to mainstream media, a lot of folks in the hip-hop community celebrated the courage and growth he expressed
in "4:44." There were think pieces written and public discourse about how dope it was for hip-hop heads to watch
their favorite artists fully mature. We weren't completely
off base. "4:44" was a far cry from the Jay that gave us
"Big Pimpin'" where he was *fuck[ing] 'em [and] leav[ing]
'em / 'Cause I don't fuckin' need 'em.* This newfound Jay-Z
was no longer the guy in "Song Cry," where a sister who
took him in when he had bad credit helped him lease a
car, and he still cheated on her. When she moved on he
explained, *I was just fuckin' 'em girls, I was gon' get right
back.* In "4:44" Jay-Z had actually changed. He was done
with those juvenile statements and ridiculous ways. But
there was a big misstep surrounding the overall public
discourse about the project. In the midst of the excitement
about his maturity and grown-man rap, we collectively
missed the chance to have a more nuanced understanding
about what repairing harm looks like for men who spent
years hurting women. If the matured Jay-Z is finally able
to now see through a woman's eyes after so many decades
of causing pain, he and the men like him who relate to

this song need to understand that the journey isn't over after a public acknowledgment of the harm they caused. They need to repair what and who they harmed. But this is bigger than one single artist. Our collective celebration of Jay's newfound self-awareness is reflective of how too many of us run to celebrate Black men who have finally seen the light of their wrongdoings after they've done harm to Black women. As a community, before we can fully celebrate men's emotional maturity breakthroughs, we need to examine what they are doing to change their behavior. This isn't exclusive to our romantic relationships, and as my childhood friend Mark showed me— sometimes this same pattern is repeated in our platonic relationships.

I adored Mark from the moment we met in elementary school. When he advanced from regular classes to the gifted program, I bragged like I was going with him. When he got accepted into an HBCU, I bragged that my best friend was going to be a "Hillman." I didn't know Hillman wasn't real at the time; I'd never heard anyone besides the characters from *A Different World* mention an all-Black college. Mark was always teaching me something—directly and indirectly. When I was fifteen, he gave me *The Philosophy and Opinions of Marcus Garvey* to read. I let it collect dust because I knew Mark usually flew through books about Black leaders and would end up passing the info along to me anyway. Mark read it three times. This was typical of him. Sharing knowledge was his way of showing he loved you. It wasn't just me he'd school about Marcus Garvey or Madam C. J. Walker; he was known for pouring Black history into everyone on the block. We all thought he was brilliant. Mark was also handsome—six three with a low Caesar haircut, slightly crooked smile, and a Morris Chestnut complexion and body. I knew he "dated" a lot of women, but I never met any of them. "Why don't you introduce me to any of your girlfriends?" I'd tease him.

"You don't bring just anybody home to meet family—not until it's serious," he said. "I'll introduce you to someone when she becomes important enough for me to introduce you."

Well, one of his girlfriends decided she didn't give a damn about his rule.

Three years later, on an unseasonably warm afternoon in November, I was in Yonkers speed walking down Ashburton Avenue to catch a bus. I was nineteen years old at this time and home from college for a break. Since it was Sunday, if I missed this bus the next one wouldn't come for another two hours.

"Hey, Shanita!" said a loud angry voice from across the street.

"Nicole?" I said, stopping, slightly out of breath from turbo walking.

She came over to me. "I haven't seen you in years," she said, trying to disguise a weird grimace with a smile. She attempted to hug me with one hand, the other was holding a bag. I reluctantly leaned in. I recognized her from high school. Her beautiful deep-brown skin, large almond-shaped eyes, and pretty teeth hadn't changed much. She was a little thicker in all the right places and her doobie was fresh from the Dominican salon. She had been a couple of grades ahead of me in school and we barely spoke, so I was surprised by this hug. "Umm, hey," I said.

I guess she could no longer handle this phony charade because she said, "Ya boy Mark ain't shit!"

I didn't know if she wanted a cosign or a fight. "Girl, what?"

"Yeah, he asked me to borrow my income tax return. After his financial aid got cut he had to move back to Yonkers and his shit was all messed up. He's been back living in Yonkers for a few months now. He's been chillin' on the block doing absolutely nothing." She waved her hand toward the corner, which was full of men looking aimless. I looked in that direction for a few seconds but then shook my head, refusing to get sucked into any parts of her drama. "Nicole, girl, I gotta run."

"But let me finish telling you about ya boy," she said cutting off my attempt to walk away. "A couple of weeks ago the cops rolled by and was messing with all them dudes and picked them up for some dumb shit. A couple of them got hit with a weed charge. Mark was released the next day but he told me he lost his job at the post office for not calling in."

I was looking over her shoulder to see if my bus was coming but Nicole snatched my attention back to her. "He lost his job?" I said, "Arrested?" This was the first time I heard that he'd lost his job. I spoke with Mark only a few weeks ago and realized there was a lot he wasn't telling me.

"That's why I gave him five thousand dollars," Nicole said. "I actually need it, and when he said he was going to pay me back with his unemployment I didn't really believe him...but I believed in him. I knew he would get back on his feet eventually. Plus I know it's hard to get back up when you've been knocked down...even the smart ones need time to figure their shit out."

"Nicole, this is a lot. I'm sorry you went through this but it's November and you're talking about something that happened during last tax season. You're stopping me out of the blue to do what exactly? And I don't really have time for this convo, girl. I'm trying to catch my bus." Then it occurred to me. "Wait...I know you don't think I'm about to pay—"

"I'm not expecting you to pay me back my money,"

she said. "Shanita, to be honest I'm not expecting him to pay me back my money either at this point. I'm just saying you need to check ya friend. He's really out here fucked up. Been spiraling ever since he had to leave school and lost his job. I tried to help, shit, a lot of women I know tried." Nicole shrugged and shook her head. She was tagging me in. It was my turn to try to save him.

"I really am sorry, Nicole. I'm not sure what else to say."

"There isn't much you can say to me but check ya boy," she said and crossed the street.

I walked a lot slower toward the bus but my mind was racing a million miles per hour with questions. Who do I know who can help Mark get a job? How do I get him to stop hanging on the block every day? It's not good for him. He needs to focus.

When I got on the bus, I sat down, pulled out my chunky Nokia cell, prepared to call Mark but then remembered I barely had any daytime minutes left on my phone plan. I quickly put my phone back in my fake Coach bag. I'll call him tonight. I have to show him he's not alone and that I got him.

"Nicole is a bird," he calmly said later on the phone. "She really didn't need to tell you our business. I've been meaning to get back to her, but I got shit going on." It sounded like he was talking about the weather and not five thousand dollars that he owed to a Black woman. I looked down at my phone to make sure I'd dialed the right number. I'd always known Mark as Mr. The Black Community Gotta Stick Together. How could he be out here acting like he didn't care about giving Nicole back her money? I found an excuse to get off the phone because I was furious with him.

I let a couple of days pass before I called again. "Mark, I can't shake what Nicole told me. I know she was one of many chicks who you were sleeping with but that's irrelevant. She just wanted to hold you down because she saw you out here trying to survive."

He sighed in frustration. "Nita, it's real out here. I'm trying to get another job, pay off this balance so my college can release my transcript and I can go back to school and move out of my mother's house. That's why I borrowed the money from her. I need to transfer to a new college and find another job. Being on your own and then coming back home to live with your mom at twenty-one is wild. We argue every day. She's the only woman I'm arguing with, though. I don't really have time for this nonsense with these other chicks."

I inhaled deeply, closed my eyes, and chose my words carefully. "Mark, you don't think I know how hard it is out here?"

"It's different for y'all," he shouted. "Black women don't go through it like this so, no, you don't really understand, Nita!" I couldn't do it this time.

"Mark, you're a selfish asshole! Either you changed or I never noticed it!"

"Man, whatever," he said. "What did you even call me for? To tell me about Nicole's dumbass problems like I ain't got my own?"

"I heard whispers about other shit you're doing to women...driving their cars around Yonkers with other women you're sleeping with in the passenger seat. Shit, I guess stealing wasn't too far off—cause that's damn sure what you did to Nicole by deciding to not return her money."

"Nita, what do you want from me right now, shit?" he said. "Like for real, what do you want me to tell you?"

It went on like this for another fifteen minutes. I didn't hang up but I put my phone down on my mom's kitchen table, took my glasses off, and rubbed my eyes. I didn't even realize I was crying until I felt the moisture on my cheeks. I picked up the phone for what I thought was going to be round two.

"So let me know what you're gonna do," he said in frustration.

"Do about what?"

"I guess you didn't hear me," he said. "I asked if you could put me down as an authorized user on your bank account."

"Mark, I'm out here on the bus scraping by. I don't have enough energy or money to save both of us. I wanted to check in on you since I heard you were acting out of character."

"Out of character?" he quipped angrily. "I'm out here trying to survive. My account went into check systems so I can't open up another bank account until I pay off an old balance for a checking account I used to have. My account was in the negative too long so now I have to deal with this bullshit. Cashing my unemployment check at the check cashing place is killing me in fees. What am I supposed to do?"

"For starters, you could stop dragging these Black women into your bullshit."

"Man, whatever."

"You know you aren't interested in a relationship with them. You are only focused on you, and they are only focused on you, so this leaves them uncared for altogether."

We both went silent. "Mark, I love you but I'm going to take some space. We're always going to be family, but you are walking around in the dark and you can't see who you're hitting. I can't speak for those women you are dealing with, but I know I'm going to end up trying to be your savior when I'm barely saving myself. The problem is you expect me and other Black women to operate in this capacity just because life is fucked up for you right now. You're one of the smartest men I know. I'll give you space to figure this out alone."

After an awkward silence the call was over. After three years of barely speaking our friendship was too.

The next time I saw Mark he was shopping in Cross County Shopping Center in Yonkers rocking a T-shirt that said LISTEN TO BLACK WOMEN. (I kid you not!) He was holding hands with a beautiful little girl that flashed a cute little crooked smile that matched his. I was shopping with our mutual friend Mika and we noticed him at the same time. I stared at him as he smiled and held hands with the little girl. He noticed us and walked toward our direction. "Did you and Mark ever patch things up?" Mika whispered through tight lips.

"Nope," I said. "I'm fine with that. He's manipulative and uses Black women because he knows we will always be there."

"I don't know if he does that anymore, Nita. He's like a different man since he had his daughter. I mean he's in a relationship with his daughter's mom and even stopped scamming women out of their 401(k)."

"MIKA, WHAT?"

She laughed and whispered for me to keep my voice down. "I'll tell you that story later, but he's chilling now so you should give him another chance."

When Mark approached us, he hugged Mika and then awkwardly tried to lean in and hug me too. I stepped back and waved instead. "Good to see you, Nita," he said as he rubbed Mika's arm and walked away.

"You are so hard on brothers, Nita," Mika said laughing. "Mark is cool now and that's still not enough for you?" We continued to shop but neither of us mentioned Mark again. The truth was Mika was right. Simply learning that Mark "stopped" doing bad things to Black women wasn't enough for me.

When it comes to Black women, there is always an expectation that we should be happy that a person stopped treating us badly. Regardless of the crime, the abuse, the toxicity of what they did, we are supposed to offer immediate forgiveness no matter the offense or harm caused. Mika never mentioned if Mark repaid any of those women for the money he took, or if he did anything at all to address the ways he hurt and humiliated them. Whether it's in our relationships, friendships, or family ties, there is always a presumption that Black women will be waiting with open arms to forgive you no matter how much harm you cause. You could burn our house down and apologize for it and the world would expect us to simply move on. But what about addressing how that fire harmed us? What about the house we lost? The truth is, a restorative framework is needed because Black women deserve more than apologies for the ways we are harmed. We deserve to have the depth of our harm fully considered and actionable steps taken to restore what we lost.

Restorative justice is a process and framework typically applied in communities that seek to handle crime, harm, and offenses without relying on punitive interventions like prison and arrest. It requires a person to repair the harm they caused before they can be reintegrated back into the community.

Restorative justice requires a harm-repairing stage, in addition to an apology or a person taking verbal responsibility for wrongdoing. The framework is rooted in Indigenous cultures and how they deal with offense, and it has resurfaced in conversations around prison abolition. The process allows a person to grow from their mistakes and openly acknowledge exactly how much pain they caused without escaping the most important step: making whole what they broke. It operates from a premise that restoration is necessary and desired by both the offender and person harmed. For instance, a harm-repairing stage for my friend Mark could have included him at least returning some of the money he borrowed and listening to the women explain exactly how his actions caused them pain and disrupted their lives.

The song "4:44" and most of the subsequent public discussions surrounding it failed to mention anything about restoring the harm that Jay-Z caused in his early years and later against his wife. All the women these men developed relationships with before they could "see the world through their eyes," because they were unable to emotionally connect are owed restoration. It's similar to what the expectations would consist of if you broke an expensive vase at a friend's dinner party after having too much to drink. You would be responsible for replacing what you broke. Apologizing profusely and offering a PhD-level analysis on why you consumed too much alcohol may help your friend empathize with you and accept your apology, but if you don't take your contrition a step further and replace the expensive vase, you will not receive another invitation to their next cocktail party. Reintegration—as it's called within a restorative justice framework—requires restoration for what was "broken." When a person impacted allows reintegration without restoring what was broken, it doesn't require full responsibility from the person who caused the harm.

A lot of Black women are more susceptible to allowing reintegration before there has been restoration if the person who caused the harm was a Black man we loved. This is even more true for our sisters who are ride-or-die chicks. Part of the ride-or-die chick's mode of operation is to act as a savior of broken men. The Black men who are incapable of emotionally connecting to us because they can't see the world through our eyes are not somebody a ride or die would avoid, it's somebody she would try to rescue. She doesn't disregard the brother, she attempts to educate him repeatedly. She performs countless acts of intellectual labor trying to get him to understand basic things about Black womanhood. The less he sees the ride or die, the more she does for him. She embarks on this rescue mission knowing that it may take more than one attempt. When and if the man does graduate from "Song Cry" to "4:44," she accepts that as her reward and a return on her "investment"—even if it's not until he is almost half a century old.

Sisters who have rejected ride-or-die status aren't exempt. A lot of Black women (like myself) have deep empathy for our brothers because we have always been able to see the world through the eyes of Black men. Most Black women could write a dissertation on the plight of the Black man in the United States. For many of us, when we were radicalized and started fighting against oppression it was our brothers we had in mind. I selected criminal justice as a college major because I wanted to help "fix" a system that was unjustly incarcerating our men. I wanted to jump into the fight and protect the "endangered Black man." I was not using my profession, voice, or talent to bring attention to things like the disproportionate childbirth mortality rates or even the fact that Black women were being incarcerated at alarmingly high rates too. I used to believe my version of pro-Blackness had no room for feminism because all I saw was the world through our brothers' eyes, and I desperately tried to protect them from danger. What's more, almost none of our music nor the news covered issues specific to Black women. The Black man's plight was the plight of all Black people and even when it became too heavy of a burden to bear, I tried to carry it anyway.

Irrespective of the ways Black women are more vulnerable, this pattern hurts our community as a whole. A community that doesn't push for a deeper level of accountability will only recycle pain. Hurt people hurt other people. It's hard to fully heal without a deep inventory of your wounds and having actionable steps implemented by the person who hurt you can help the healing journey. Healed people can help heal people. Not everyone that caused harm in our community needs to be canceled or banished forever. For some there can be a path to restoration, but only the person who was harmed gets to decide what, if anything, that path could look like.

As for the men who have a late-in-life awakening about the emotional damage they caused Black women, we fail those who were harmed when we don't hold our applause and push the men to work on a restoration plan for those who paid the ugly price for their awakening. I feel a complicated set of emotions when the Black men I love embark on a path of emotional maturity and self-reflection that was paved on the backs of Black women. On one hand, I rejoice when brothers reach a level of maturity where they reflect on the harm they caused Black women and decide to do better moving forward. In fact, a lot of Black women love this for them and we know that it can translate into healthier relationships with us, platonic or otherwise. Yet, if you talk to a Black woman who was in a relationship of any kind with these men before they began self-reflecting, healing, and unlearning, they will show you the emotional scars he inflicted. While some women may choose to give them grace and room to repair the harm because they lacked the skills to understand the damage they caused, it doesn't excuse bad behavior—especially considering some of the men were manipulative, cold-hearted, emotionally unavailable womanizers, or worse. Watching a brother transition from an emotional terrorist of Black women into a celebrated example of maturity and growth is complex. To be completely happy that he arrived at this place of emotional maturity and ignore the casualties along the way is to knowingly accept an unspoken social contract that stipulates Black women's pain is acceptable collateral damage as long as the person who harmed her grew. It's time to correct this mindset.

Despite the missed opportunity to explore a deeper narrative, "4:44" did in fact highlight critical aspects of healing and reminded us that sometimes we just have to start fresh. In "4:44" Jay told us he *suck[s] at love* and needs a *do-over*. The conversation around "4:44" needs a do-over. It should be resumed and center on why our community struggles with affording Black women repair before restoration. When we don't reflect on the cost of such an expensive healing journey, we make a decision about who is disposable in our community and who deserves unmitigated grace. Reflecting on the "cost" of this healing is only a preliminary step. Political activist and scholar Angela Davis said, "You have to act as if it were possible to radically transform the world. And you have to do it all the time."

If we want to radically transform our communities and dismantle the social contracts that are detrimental to Black women, then we have to radically transform how we think about harm, accountability, and restoration. We have to truly believe that it's even possible for our community to reframe our thinking on this. Both individually and as a collective Black community, we can no longer adhere to the unspoken narrative that Black women's suffering is acceptable collateral damage for broken men. Nor can the world continue to operate as if our grace is so endless that nothing more than a public confession of one's sin is required for an eternal relationship. Black women got ninety-nine gifts but being Jesus ain't one.

5

WAP

*If she want to be a freak and sell it on the weekends /
It's none of your business.*

—Salt-N-Peppa

In the summer of 2020, amid the sweltering heat of August, and on the tail of a global racial reckoning amplified by a pandemic, two women snatched the world's attention by talking about their wet-ass pussies. Rappers Cardi B and Megan Thee Stallion released their instant hit, "WAP," and the flood gates flew open. The song, a four-minute track where the rappers take turns describing their sexual talents and need for men who can keep up, has amassed over 1 billion streams on Spotify alone, and the video has been viewed on YouTube over 450 million times. "WAP" was a trending topic on social media, group chats were lighting up, and think pieces were published immediately after the song was released. One writer called the song a feminist anthem: "As Gen Zers and millennials, we should be focused on how 'WAP' has become a cultural touchstone and what it means for the feminist movement."

The impact of "WAP" transcended generations. Those of us who were still in high school and had no business rapping along with Lil' Kim when she was talking about taking it in the ass and her bomb-ass pussy felt like we were transported back in time. In 1996, Kim dropped her album *Hard Core*. Back then, Kim was the young girl from Brooklyn lyrically holding her own at a time when hip-hop revolved around male New York rappers. Both the song and video for "WAP" reminded '90s New York hip-hop heads of Kim, and it felt great to relive those moments. The colorful hair, the way they danced, and of course the unapologetic way Cardi and Meg centered their sexual desires. It felt good to see traces of Kim's influence. She helped create the lane that Cardi and Meg were now soaring in, and the girls are indeed flying.

Prior to "WAP," both Cardi and Meg were well-known and talented artists, but the song helped their careers advance to another level. Meg went on to score four Grammy nominations in 2021 and Cardi became the first female rapper to reportedly have five number-one hits on Billboard's Top 100. The release of "WAP" was epic. Still, the song wasn't met with total celebration. Not every Black woman was excited. Some did not find lyrics like *I don't cook, I don't clean / But let me tell you how I got this ring* empowering for women. My best friend, Yenny, was one of them. Yen and I have been friends for over fifteen years. There's been times when she rubbed my back and prayed for me while I cried over a guy who broke my heart, finished her prayer, and then lovingly offered to drive to his

house with a bat. Whether she was assuring me that heart-
break won't last forever or volunteering to go beat up some
guy on my behalf, she was always sincere. Yenny from the
block is a down-to-earth type of girl who will always show
up for her crew in the name of sisterhood. This doesn't
mean Yenny dishes out her cosign when she doesn't agree
with something all in the name of "girl power."

The first time Yenny and I listened to "WAP" together,
we didn't make it beyond the first couple of seconds before
her face told me she didn't like the song. When the beat
dropped, and you heard the hook, *There's some hoes in this
house,* I immediately smiled and thought Cardi and Meg
sampling the original song from DJ Frank Ski was their
way of reclaiming the title of "hoe." By the time Cardi said,
Certified freak, seven days a week, I was ready to bodyroll.
Yen, on the other hand, sighed, rolled her eyes, shook her
head, and adjusted her glasses. This was classic Yenny. She
is always perfectly clear and honest about how she feels.
Even if she wanted to hide what she was truly thinking,
her facial expressions would expose her.

"Okay, so why don't you like the song?" I asked.

"For many reasons," she said. "I do believe in women
owning their sexuality and you already know I'm not a
prude." We both laughed when she said that. Fifteen years
of friendship comes with stories. Stories that will stay in

the vault, but yeah, my girl is anything but a prude. "Listen, I've done my share of things, just google me," she continued, "but I just don't believe you have to be this raunchy to express yourself sexually. I feel like it's an oxymoron to talk about a song being empowering to women when it opens up with *'hoes in this house.'* These are opposing views. The entire point of owning your sexuality is so that people are not referring to you as a hoe and putting you down for what you're doing sexually. Plus, for Black women, and women of color in general, these are stereotypes that we have to contend with when we are fighting to be respected for our minds."

I paused. Even though I didn't share her same sentiment it was worth considering. "I hear you, Yen, but as Black women, we get to reclaim our sexuality in whatever way we choose because of all the years we weren't able to," I said.

She nodded to acknowledge my point. "There is this view of us as being nothing more than these overly sexualized beings with these wet-ass pussies. This goes back generations for us. So for them to say to the world, yea this is who we are—it feels unnecessary because we've worked for years to say we are more than that. Yes, I'm clutching my proverbial pearls." She started to snap her fingers in the way Black folks do when we are trying to remember something. "There's a lyric in the song, that's about a car but I can't think of what it is...."

I excitedly chimed in, "Ohhhhh, when my girl Meg said, *'Ask for a car while you ride that dick.'*"

"Yeah, that's it," Yen said. "Shanita, that's part of why I have a problem with the song—why do we have to use sex to get what we want from a man? I buy my own stuff. If her message was to enjoy yourself and buy your own shit I would be more open to it, but it's the exchange of sex for gifts that's taking it over the edge for me. As a feminist and boss this is just a hard no for me. Don't get me wrong, we should never look down on women who express themselves sexually. Beyoncé expresses sexuality in her music, performances, and look, while it may be different from Cardi and Meg, it still comes from a place of understanding that pleasure is a good thing. I appreciate that Beyoncé is subtle and I can still pump my favorite music even with the kids around because they don't know she's talking about sex."

"Yen, is *'Driver roll up the partition please / I don't want you seeing Yoncé on her knees'* a discrete line to you?" I asked. "There is nothing subtle about the song 'Partition.'" I couldn't help but laugh. "Yen, she is talking about sucking dick in the back of the car and asking her driver to give her a lil privacy. I mean, I ain't mad at her for giving head in the car, but that ain't discrete."

We both laughed and exchanged knowing looks that neither of us had to explain.

"I'm just saying my thirteen-year-old daughter might not instantly catch that reference," she said, "not as quickly as she would when a rapper says, *'Give me everything you got for this wet ass pussy.'*"

"I feel you though, Yen. I just appreciate that this song even exists. I like watching younger Black women who are free about what they want sexually and don't give a damn about being labeled anything."

Honestly though, I appreciate sexual freedom because I missed out on my hoe phase and I simply don't have the knees anymore to be in these streets. When I was younger, I was too worried about what men thought of me. I wanted to be that good and smart girl and that mattered more than my own sexual desires. That good girl mentality stayed with me well into adulthood. There was no time in life where sex was about what I wanted and needed because I didn't know that it could. By the time I did start having sex, it was done purely to please the man I was with.

"Girl, I was a grown-ass married woman and had only had an orgasm once and that was back when I was in college," I said, shaking my head in disgust. Yen's eyes opened wide. Shame had kept me from sharing that with her about my past.

"That has just never ever been my testimony, girl. I don't know that life," she said. "I want to start a GoFundMe for you or something because I feel so bad."

"Oh, baby, don't feel too bad for me," I said. "I have since reclaimed my time."

We laughed. She knew all about my post–married life escapades. "Oh, I bet," she said in between laughs.

Yenny and I concluded our conversation the way we usually do since the pandemic started: "Okay, girl, love you, but I'm about to hop on a Zoom meeting."

It's always interesting and engaging when talking with Black women about their reactions to "WAP." Many seem to either love the song or hate it, or are indifferent to it altogether. Men on the other hand are a different story. I find a lot of my conversations with men about it completely maddening and not worth engaging. A bunch of men sitting around talking about what's an "acceptable" form of feminism and what constitutes women's "empowerment" is almost as infuriating as a gang of white folks getting together to decide what Black liberation should entail. In both instances it implies a perceived ownership over said group and it operates from a position of superiority. If two grown women decide they want to write a love letter to their pussy and tell the whole world they want to swallow dick, that is what they get to do. Men don't get to weigh in on what we do with our bodies in any form. They don't get to determine what is empowering for us. They do not get to make decisions about how or if we talk about sex. How some random man feels about that is completely irrelevant because I'm vehemently against policing a woman's body in any form. I want men to mind their own damn business. I want women to mind their own damn business. It's not about what you want for her. It's about what she wants, and if dick is the thing, then so be it.

We need to move beyond debating whether it's empowering for women to explicitly talk about sex or have multiple partners—which is what part of the collective discussion around "WAP" developed into. Instead, we need to interrogate our own framework around sex as individuals and get honest about how much societal expectations around gender norms are influencing it.

I love hearing Black women being free about sex and explicitly stating what they want. Sis, I want you to shun respectability politics in all forms. As a collective, we need to demolish every notion that suggests we modify our behavior to appeal to dominant groups, whether that's men or white people in general. Black women deserve freedom to express themselves sexually without having to justify this to anyone. The goal of the sex-positive movement is freedom: even if that freedom includes being ethically nonmonogamous, having multiple sex partners while screaming about your wet-ass pussy, or being a grown woman with an OnlyFans page. It deconstructs the patriarchal control of sex and sexuality. However, true power only happens when you are operating from a place of honesty. You have to be candid with yourself about your sexual expressions and experiences. This entails being clear on whether you can handle emotional attachments that may be formed and possibly not reciprocated. In terms of women having safe sex with multiple partners, I'm the girl cheering from the bench. I'm also long past viewing sex as something I do to please my partner. Not having an orgasm during sex is now a deal breaker for me. To remix my girl Meg, he can keep that car if he ain't got good dick. But emotionally, I can't handle having sex outside of a monogamous relationship. I need to feel an emotional connection to my partner in order to feel safe enough to have sex, and monogamy helps me better establish this. I'm self-aware enough to not engage in sexual experiences that are outside my emotional capacity. None of this negates how I feel about women who are able to, and choose to, operate in a different capacity. Black women must free ourselves enough to ask the tough questions. Do you have the capacity—emotional and otherwise—to welcome love and partnership from multiple people in your life or do you want your partner to know that you're down for whatever (aht aht! I see you, ride-or-die chick).

Don't get it twisted, the sister that appears to be more sexually conservative isn't always operating from a place of self-awareness either. Some sisters hate "WAP" and any form of unapologetic and open expression of sexuality because they were taught being "the good girl" will land you the coveted prize of marriage. The good girl takes shots at the Cardis and Megs of the world by posting images on social media rocking a turtleneck and cardigan with a caption like #ClassyNotTrashy. She will not have sex outside of monogamy simply because she wants to appear more chaste in the eyes of a man. Hell, she probably cringes at the use of the word "pussy" because "good girls don't talk like that." Listen, sis, you can rock your turtleneck all year-round and not have sex until you get married in an effort to be a good girl, but is that what you really want? Or is it what you have been taught? Do you hate "WAP" because you were taught that appearing chaste will get you a ring but here you are single and lonely while a former stripper turned rap sensation, wife, and mother earned the "reward" you're still "working" for? Do you resent any form of women being overtly sexual because you long for the freedom to do the same but your heteronormative, patriarchal views won't allow you to? You don't have to tell me, but at least tell yourself the truth.

You know you're doing it right when you can ask yourself the tough questions and dig down deep for the answers. Most of us have to pull out the journals or spend long wine nights with friends before we can get to the bottom of what sexual freedom looks like for us. Sexual liberation looks like understanding our truth. It looks like us no longer conforming to standards around sexuality that don't reflect who we truly want to be. Which is what Black women deserve.

6

MY SISTER'S KEEPER

*Is solace anywhere more comforting than that in
the arms of a sister?*

— Alice Walker

Black sisterhood has always been powerful enough to love us back to life when the world killed our spirits. When fear is holding us hostage, it's other Black women who show up with the ransom. We pull up armed with the words to free our sisters from self-doubt and destructive self-talk. This is who we are and this is what our sisterhood provides. Sometimes, however, when one of our own is wylin out, our sisters call us in. "Calling in" is the complete opposite of "calling out." Calling in is a way of correcting a behavior in order to make them and our community better. Calling somebody out is dragging them in public with no regard for your relationship with them or how they receive what you have to say. For example, having a difficult conversation with one of your girls about the way they are upholding patriarchal standards about sex and control by judging other women based on their number of sex partners is a way of calling that friend in. Calling in is rooted in love and protection. It's reserved for those we value. None of us are above needing to be called in, even Black women. We are long overdue for a call in around some cishet Black women's homophobia. To our queer sisters, I understand how exhausting it can get when you have to constantly do the emotional labor of teaching folks in community with you about their homophobia. Despite how frequently some cishet Black women adopt queer lingo and have flourishing platonic relationships with queer sisters, there is still more we need to do for our liberation efforts to include all Black women. The goal of this chapter is to do some of the heavy lifting for you, sis. Trust me, helping some cishet Black women see our own homophobia is definitely a lift.

It's hard to imagine that cishet Black women who are known to fight against misogynoir and oppression could also contribute to the harm of an even more marginalized group. Especially when said group is composed of Black queer women who have always been at the forefront of women's rights movements. One would imagine that those who know the pain of bigotry would recognize when they are the very ones failing others in this area, but the truth is some cishet Black women are incredibly toxic to our queer sisters and don't get held accountable for this often enough. It's important for cishet Black women to be more aligned with our queer sisters by recognizing the privileges afforded to us by our cisness and our straightness. Equally important, attitudes against queer and trans folks go against the list of rights afforded to all women.

Black women need each other in this fight against patriarchy and racism—none of us can do it alone. Although
our sisterhood is predicated on far more than just war-
ring against subjugation, it's certainly for our collective
well-being to stand together against oppression. Standing together entails more than just straight Black women
having relationships with queer sisters. Standing together
looks like consciously challenging yourself to reframe your
thinking so that heterosexuality is not the only (or standard) sexual orientation and that you value and respect
their romantic partnerships. Standing together includes
doing things like making room for their full queer identity
in our friendships. Standing together also requires cishet
Black women to show up around issues of homophobia and
transphobia, even when they are subtle and not physically
violent. Otherwise you are more than likely devaluing your
queer sisters.

Most of the time, homophobia and transphobia are
avenues for some men to engage in dangerous physical
violence against women and queer people. Similar to our
conversation on measuring against extremes, too often
microaggressions don't even register as toxic when they're
outside the parameters of physical violence. Dirty looks at
queer couples and transphobic jokes can seem like online
debate topics until someone has lost their life to physical

violence, typically perpetrated by cis men. Darnell Moore, activist and author of *No Ashes in the Fire* and whose work centers Black queer lives, unpacked the scope of violence against Black lesbians in an article for *Out* magazine. His article addressed the question, "Why do we still have so much violence directed at queer women of color?" Moore wrote about the murder of two Black lesbians and noted, "But the murder of Shani and Ray-Ray illuminated a particular type of everyday violence that is both racialized and gendered, a type of violence that evidences the consequences of sexism and homo-antagonism precisely aimed at Black women (who love other women)." When cishet Black women engage in casual homophobia and transphobia and don't get called in for it, people's lives are at stake. Because it's usually not as physically violent and life-threatening, we often find the public scrutiny of the gender and sexuality of others acceptable or do not challenge it. But how many times have we suffered from that same scrutiny? This is especially true of those of us who have been hip-hop heads since we were teens. Hip-hop did not create homophobia or transphobia, but it certainly reflects the attitudes of the country the genre was birthed in and therefore more deeply entrenches anti-queer ideals. You don't have to go far to see this in the United States. The massive charge to ban books written by queer authors and the attack on queer children by imposing legislature that prohibits discussions about sexual identity and gender in the classrooms is a clear demonstration of the United States' history of anti-LGBTQIA+ sentiment. Hip-hop takes its cues from the United States and some of us who are engulfed in hip-hop culture are unconsciously using it as an odometer for what does and does not constitute violence against the queer community. It excuses us from having to interrogate our own non-physically violent behaviors and practices that also contribute to harming queer sisters. Many straight Black women have meaningful friendships with queer sisters and are still homophobic and reinforce heteronormative thinking without realizing it. This thinking permeates our encounters with our queer sisters whether we share space with them or not.

Despite the strong friendships I have with queer Black women, I've been guilty of this and my friend Tina, who is gay, suffered because of it. We were having brunch one Sunday, scrolling social media when the rumor mill about my celebrity crush kicked into overtime. "If I see this picture floating online one more time I'm going to scream," I said to Tina. I leaned over the table and handed Tina my phone so she could see the picture of my crush appearing flirty with another man. "If one more person comments on this picture implying that they are a couple I'm just gonna pass out."

She laughed and playfully made a sad face. "Aww, maybe you need to break up with your boo in ya head," she said. "Is he still on your vision board with the label 'Black Love' scrolled across the top?"

I snatched my phone back.

"Girl," she said, "maybe you spoke Black love into his life, 'cause he looks happy."

I rolled my eyes. "If those rumors are true then that's a waste of a good Black dick. I mean damn, how is his fine ass gay?" I laughed but Tina didn't this time. We ate the rest of our boozy brunch in an awkward silence. I assumed the tapered conversation was a result of the endless mimosas. I was getting full and tipsy, a combination that made me sleepy. Tina was getting annoyed and tipsy, a combination that usually made her talk slick but she was silent. Brunch ended the way it always did. We split the bill, hugged, and left the restaurant going in our separate directions. Days later we picked up like nothing ever happened. We chatted about going shopping and about anything and nothing at all.

It took several years, some personal growth, honest self-reflection, listening to queer women express their struggles with homophobia in hip-hop, and another girls' brunch for my friend Tina to finally receive the long over-due apology from me. I told her that what I'd said about my celebrity crush years ago at brunch was toxic, homophobic, and disrespectful. I acknowledged that stating if my crush was a complete waste of a good dick if he was gay assumes that anyone outside of a heterosexual relationship is a waste and that's just wrong. I'd implied to my friend that she is also a waste since she's gay, and I said I never wanted to make her feel that way. I was embarrassed and genuinely felt awful. Tina was far more gracious in her response to my apology than I deserved or expected.

"Nita, I know you are generally a champion for Black women, so I gave you a pass for that. I was pissed because that's trash on so many levels. Gay Black women have so many fights at once. Sometimes I go to a family gathering and have to argue with the drunk relative who is ranting about how life is easy for the gays because we got equal rights and Black folks don't. Like I'm not a whole ass Black woman who is also gay. These goofy folks can't imagine how ridiculous they sound, like a person can't be both gay and Black." She chuckled, rolled her eyes, and took another sip of her mimosa. "Ignoring the folks who don't understand that concept is a lot easier than risking physical confrontations with men who think I'm destroying the Black family." This time there was no chuckle. "I've had arguments damn near become physical when a brother screamed at me and my partner about how we are destroying the Black community cause we're gay. I've had to police my own damn tone while he screamed in my face because it felt like he might swing on me if I didn't.

"He wasn't some random dude walking down the street. I was at one of my girl's cookouts and one of her guy friends having one too many shots of brown liquor went from chilling to violence quick." Tina was getting angrier the more she talked about it. I sat silently and let her anger take up all the space it needed. Her final point hit me hard, "So yeah, you've said some trash shit but at least I didn't have to worry about the possibility of physical violence."

Tina's words were sobering. I never considered that I was another "battle" she had to fight. There were so many layers I needed to peel back from my mindset about homosexuality to fully see myself. Why did it take so many years for me to realize what I'd said to her was trash? Why didn't hearing her stories about somebody being violent toward her at a cookout enrage me more? If she'd told me some white guy had jumped in her face and said Black people are destroying this country, I would have been ready to take my earrings off and grab my Vaseline for what he did to my friend. Instead I felt nothing beyond sadness for my friend's experience. My natural instinct to protect was not activated in that moment when I learned about the violence she can face on a given day. I was ignorant to all the ways my silence made her suffer.

We hugged, split the check, and left the restaurant in our separate directions. As I walked home, I tried to start peeling back these layers; I had to interrogate some of the spaces that framed my thinking around the queer community. It started with my formative years in the Black church and seamlessly bled into my relationship with hip-hop.

My experiences in the Black church desensitized me to violence toward homosexuality. I was nine years old when my mother started sending my older brothers and me to church and Sunday school every week. Rome was eleven and Kia was thirteen. We would walk about four blocks each way in our best clothes. At the time, my mom worked two full-time jobs, so she was too tired to attend with us. We would attend Sunday school for one hour and then sit through a million-hour-long service. (Okay, it was two hours, but it felt like a lifetime to me.) I would distract myself by counting how many ladies had on big hats that week and time how long the older Black deacon in the corner could keep his eyes open (which was only for a few minutes, so he wasn't a helpful distraction). On the best days, the man behind the organ would play songs I liked and that would make church more fun. Kia typically spent most of the service peering at the large pictures all over the sanctuary and rambling to himself. I was never sure of what he was saying exactly. What I got sounded like he was playing a game of name that white man. One day when I was especially bored I moved closer to him on our pew. "Kia, what you doing?" I asked.

He pointed to the massive picture of "Jesus" on the wall that towered over the congregation. "I think that man they calling Jesus is a self-portrait of Michelangelo. Or maybe not him, but it's definitely a picture of whoever the artist was. I'm trying to think of who the artist could be." Kia could have said those words in Mandarin and they would've been just as clear to my English-speaking ass. "Huh?"

"Shanita, that is not a picture of no Jesus on the wall. Jesus ain't have blond hair and blue eyes. He had woolly hair and dark skin like us," Kia said. He was kind of loud and one of the older church ladies next to us mumbled, "These kids have no respect for anything," as she grabbed her Bible and left the pew.

"Then why is his picture up there like that," I whispered, "and everybody in here is calling him Jesus."

"Slavery," Kia said, delivering his go-to response, at the same volume. More people moved away from us but Kia continued in a tone that was usually reserved for two people at a dinner party. It was only him and the pastor speaking at that level. "White people stole Black people from Africa and took us to America and made us slaves for hundreds of years. They stole our religion too. They told us everything we knew about God before they stole us was wrong and said now you got Jesus and shackles. Then they beat everybody with whips, raped the mothers, and sold children and made everybody pick cotton in the hot sun and never paid them for hundreds of years and said it's cool cause the Bible said it's okay 'cause it's the curse of Ham so this is how Black people are supposed to be treated." Kia said all that without taking a breath.

"Who told you all this, Kia?" I whispered.

"I read books," he replied and went back to his game.

I sat there confused. I had never heard of anything more wicked in my entire life and I couldn't understand why God did not destroy those evil white people. The only reference I had of God using his power to destroy people as a form of punishment was when Pastor told us about Sodom and Gomorrah. A few Sundays before Kia taught me about slavery, Pastor told us the Bible says God burned down a whole city cause he didn't like that folks living in the city were gay. "God hates sin, and homosexuality is a sin and an abomination. Our Father is a loving God but he will also burn down a whole city to deal with this abomination like he did in Sodom and Gomorrah," the pastor yelled into the mic and the congregation cosigned. "You preaching good, Pastor!" one of the ladies sitting in the front row with the big hats yelled.

"That's the word right there. Straight from the Bible!" another yelled. The sleepy Black deacon began rocking back and forth in his seat. The organist pressed on the keys to add a dramatic flair in the background. The folks in the congregation swayed, waved their hands in the air, and leaned in harder with praise when the pastor said things like, "They have to be delivered from that demonic spirit and repent unless they want to go to hell." That Sunday I didn't count a single big hat or time any sleepy deacons. I needed to know who these "awful" people were that God would rain down fire from heaven to punish.

As the pastor continued his sermon about the gay people who had evil spirits inside them, my nine-year-old mind flashed to a scene in *The Exorcist,* a horror movie about a girl possessed by a demon. I imagined gay people walking around with their heads twisting backward, with skin that burst into flames when touched with the cross of a Catholic priest. Of course this was after they spewed vomit while their eyes rolled to the backs of their heads. I learned God wanted gay people to change their lives, otherwise he would make them suffer for an eternity. "There was no coming back from hell!" the pastor shouted.

My mom stopped sending us to church three years later but the muddled messages I'd conceived were already solidified: God burned down gay cities but didn't let any fire fall from the sky for four hundred years of slavery. Damn, being gay must be the worst thing you can do to you. Without realizing it, I'd internalized the idea that queerness was wrong and worthy of punishment, which was the root of my comment years later about my potentially gay celebrity crush being a waste.

At twelve years old, I went from listening to violent messages about gay people in church to falling in love with a genre with lyrics dripping with homophobia. After years of listening to violent rhetoric about gay people over a dope beat in church, there was no level of homophobia a rapper could spew that would make me raise my eyebrows, or even anger me. Especially if it came from a talented charismatic rapper that I felt personally connected to, like DMX.

When DMX died in 2021, I was heartbroken, but some of the queer people I knew expressed vastly different reactions to his death. For me, a writer from his hometown in Yonkers, X was the local hero who modeled how to use vulnerability in art. He never hid himself from the public. Every complicated and seemingly contradictory layer was on full display. At a concert, the man could go from literally growling like a dog and talking about killing you one minute to leading the audience in prayer the next. A DMX concert didn't feel like an ordinary performance—it felt like watching a troubled but talented man publicly peel back layers and reveal himself.

His layers blinded me—no matter how gritty and dark his songs got—all I could see was the softer side of him, his vulnerability, and I loved it. In my hood there were men just as talented as him; X was just another guy from around the way that could rap. Every city in the United States has them but he soared from the block to the top of the music charts, and I was proud of him. He wrote his way out of the hood and made me believe words could be wings.

When the song "Where the Hood At" was released in 2003, it was a breaking point for some of my queer friends with X. In the song X talks trash about guys he had beef with: *Last I heard, y'all niggas was having sex with the same sex... How y'all niggas gonna explain fucking a man?* And as if he wasn't clear enough, he raps, *I show no love to homo thugs / Empty out reloaded and throw mo' slugs.* The video has men dressed in feminine attire walking around in the midst of a large crowd that is mocking them with a barrage of homophobic and transphobic gestures and signaling that their own behavior was appropriate and even trendy.

That song may have been the breaking point for some

people, but X certainly wasn't the only rapper with homophobic content. Eminem has never given a damn about
using the F-word in his music. Offset from the three-man
group Migos rapped on a YFN Lucci track, *I cannot vibe
with the queers.* Rapper DaBaby paused his performance
at the Rolling Loud concert in July of 2021 to go on a
homophobic rant where he said, "Fellas if you ain't sucking
dick in the parking lot, put your cell phone lighters up."
While DMX maintained his star status despite his open
homophobia, we now have Black Twitter, journalists, writers, and content creators with large internet platforms who
bring immediate attention to these stories. This serves
as a way to hold artists accountable and at times it has
resulted in financial repercussions. After DaBaby slandered
the LGBTQIA+ community, venues canceled his concerts.
The problem is not that we fail to call out homophobia in
hip-hop or in our community at large, the issue is that it's
usually the physically violent vitriol spewed by men in hip-
hop that has served as the odometer to measure toxicity
and homophobia.

That standard allowed me to operate as if I wasn't harmful to our queer sisters. I couldn't imagine that I too could
ever be destructive in any way toward queer sisters because
I was never threatening their personal safety. When the bar
becomes a beating or shooting, it's harder to recognize the

mental, emotional, and social forms of homophobia that cisgender, heterosexual Black women engage in. Measuring toxicity against the vilest acts of homophobia displayed by some men makes some cishet Black women less likely to even hear ourselves when we are spewing microaggressions toward our queer sisters and less likely to be challenged on it. As a cishet Black woman, I am challenging us to do better and raise the bar. We have to protect all our queer sisters. Black trans women are killed and physically attacked for simply existing. According to data on violence against trans communities, "Black transgender women were more likely to be physically attacked for being transgender." Data reported by the Human Rights Campaign identified "2021 as the most violent year on record since HRC began tracking these crimes in 2013." This data also indicates that "the majority of these people were Black and Latina trans women."

Our queer sisters are facing harm and danger at multiple levels and they deserve to be protected from it all: even microaggressions. Most of us have had to explain to a white person that microaggressions aren't just examples of marginalized people being "too sensitive." We fully understand that despite what the name implies, there is nothing "micro" about the aggressions. The acts in question may occur in smaller doses throughout a day but they are rooted in aggression, bigotry, or stereotypical notions. Repeated occurrences can feel like a constant drop of water falling on the same spot on your face. One drop every once in a while is annoying. Prolonged drops in the same spot with no end in sight is torture. We understand how this feels but often struggle to see when we are the conduits of countless microaggressions toward our queer sisters.

When cishet Black woman refuse to see our queer sisters' full identity we are being way too similar to those fake white feminist allies who want to dismantle our Blackness. Cishet Black women don't always come out and say things like "I don't see you as gay, I just see you as a Black woman," but when we refuse to do things like engage in conversations with our queer friends about their love interests, we convey a similar message. We shop with our queer sisters, hang out with them, run our mouths with them about everything under the sun but somehow we don't express the slightest interest in who they might be partnered with, or want to be partnered with, or hell, even just dating. We don't show any interest at all in their love. Which is unlike how we center and celebrate heterosexual love, sex, and relationships. When straight couples like football player Russell Wilson and singer Ciara, or entrepreneur Ayesha

Curry and her husband Stephen Curry post loving messages to each other on social media we yasssss girl it up with #BlackLove in those comment sections, and we don't even know them. Meanwhile, some of us don't say a peep or celebrate the love lives of our queer friends. Some cishet Black women have moved beyond gross and blatant statements, like telling a queer friend that a celebrity crush is a waste of a good Black dick if he's gay, but are still being harmful by pretending they don't see their friend's queer identity.

Some of us are still refusing to do basic things like use our friends' preferred pronouns when they explicitly ask us to. For some cishet Black women this isn't just the occasional, accidental misgendering of one of our trans sisters, followed by an apology and quick correction. It's the repeated refusal to use one's correct pronouns but not considering yourself transphobic simply because you speak against the murders of Black trans women online. Speaking against the murder of Black trans women is the most basic thing we can do as productive, socially conscious members of the Black community. It's a basic way of acknowledging that our trans sisters deserve to live. They deserve an existence that's not just about fighting or survival. They deserve our love and full embrace of who they are.

Cishet Black women cannot allow the physical violence

inflicted by some men to become the standard we measure our love against. It's a low-ass bar to follow and it sends the message that there is an acceptable level of toxicity our queer sisters should endure. To undo this, we have to understand that cishet Black women can have relationships with queer Black women and still harm them. Cisgender, heterosexual Black women have spent decades of our lives fighting against misogynoir in hip-hop and oppression in general, yet this does not make us incapable of absorbing the toxic homophobia engulfing our society. Acknowledging this is just the first step. Once we realize we have been toxic and harmful toward our queer sisters we have to find ways to repair the harm we caused. Which isn't unlike what we ask of the brothers who come to their "4:44" later in life. For me this looks like using my words, time, and platform to fight for our queer sisters. We must push ourselves to unlearn toxic traits so that we are never another battle a queer sister has to fight. Repair also means holding other cishet Black women accountable—which of course, won't be easy, especially if a sister isn't ready to change and grow. For the well-being of Black women as a whole, it's necessary to take care of, acknowledge, and love hard on queer sisters, and vice-versa. Even when this means lovingly calling each other in.

7

A HEALING

We identify our triggers so we can heal.
—Ty Alexander-Williams

I t's been over ten years since my car was repossessed but the vision of it being taken away is still my first thought whenever I accidently walk out of a store to the wrong parking spot and find a blank space where my car should have been. The grip of a traumatic experience doesn't have an expiration date. The trauma I experienced after an unexpected job loss later manifested in the form of excessive "grinding." My success has been cultivated out of my fear and trauma around economic instability. From the outside, I look like a woman who taught online courses in two separate countries; juggled multiple speaking engagements; did freelance writing for multiple publications; provided consultations on mental health to corporations; and landed the competitive Soros Justice Fellowship that required me to write the hell out of a proposal, outshine hundreds of other applicants, and then dazzle an entire panel during a Zoom interview. I juggled this career and obtained my fellowship during a pandemic that disproportionately impacted Black people. If I allowed you a closer look, you would see my ambition is the byproduct of high-functioning but often debilitating anxiety stemming from a history of financial hardships: all of which is a form of PTSD according to the Center for Financial Social Work. I'm terrified of ever having to relive the days when an unexpected Hulu and Netflix payment withdrawal could damn near empty my bank account. I'm so haunted by this that even when I'm doing well financially, I still take on multiple projects to increase my revenue with little regard for my mental health or self-care.

In hip-hop, there are countless songs written to celebrate women like me, who appear to be grinding. They love to sing about us securing the bag. Gucci Mane's "Bad Bitch" felt like a tribute to me when he said, *Got a taxi service and a beauty parlor / And go to school, she a Rhodes scholar.* Sis is booked and busy! Cardi B can always amp me up to juggle like fifty-eleven jobs with lines like *Dropped two mix tapes in six months / What bitch working as hard as me?* in her instant hit "Bodak Yellow." Long before Cardi or even Gucci, Lil' Kim gave me an evergreen anthem with her verse on Junior M.A.F.I.A.'s "Get Money" and the line *fuck niggas, get money was my fuel.* It's worth noting that in this song both Kim and Biggie have super-problematic lines that don't deserve to be amplified. It's strictly the "fuck niggas" line that stands out for me. When I don't want to reflect on the fact that even when I've longed for romantic partnerships, I still deprioritized them in my life to focus on my money, that line becomes my go-to-mantra. There is always a hip-hop song available to camouflage your trauma when your personal goal is to create as much revenue as you can—self-nurturing be damned.

It's not just the music that hypes up my grind, my community loves it. On any given day I will receive some version of this from my family or friends: "Shanita is hot on these streets" or "Shanita is killing the game." My personal favorite comes from other Black women. "Okay, I see you, sis." What I never allowed them to see were the times I opened my laptop and stared at my screen for hours without writing and barely breathing because the thought of having to formulate words for the public meant the possibility of failing, which could mean being broke again. When I spend the day struggling to breathe, thoughts of all the work I missed rob me at night. Anxiety-filled days bleed into sleepless nights and when I finally erupt with productivity, the world celebrates my grind.

We shouldn't have an issue with the people or music that celebrate us. There is nothing wrong with the Black women who praise me for having fifty-eleven projects simultaneously. They don't see what is driving my actions. The problem is my inclination to respond to the trauma by creating more work with little regard for my well-being.

We don't always recognize some of our actions as trauma responses—mine is about money—but healing journeys are personal, and we all have to be able to identify our own. I've been celebrated for my ambition and the affirmations I receive from other Black women bring me joy, but the praise also allows me to hide in broad daylight. It allows me to reinforce this behavior and prevents me from digging deeper to find a way out. We must know our trauma responses well in order to develop healthy strategies to heal them.

Misidentified trauma-based responses don't always present as something as extreme as an inability to stop overworking. They can vary in how excessively they present. Sometimes you will have a lighthearted response to a very traumatic incident. I learned this after one right-swipe on the Bumble dating app that turned into several easy-flowing dates with Tyrone.

Tyrone and I had an effortless chemistry. Talking to somebody you met on a dating app can feel like a job interview—especially considering most guys on dating apps refuse to actually read your profile. The first few conversations are dry and robotic: How long have you been single? What do you do for a living? Do you have any kids? What are you looking for in a relationship? Tyrone and I skipped that stage and instead spent most of our first few conversations debating whether Biggie was the greatest rapper of all time. Tyrone was ready to die on that hill but I wasn't convinced. Despite how great of a storyteller Biggie was, there was no way Tyrone would convince me that a rapper with only two albums is the GOAT, but I was happy to indulge him.

These types of lighthearted debates were a stark contrast to the whirlwind we were living through in the summer of 2020, which was around the time when Tyrone and I met. The country was grieving from loss due to the pandemic and working through a new normal in the midst of fighting against a massive spike in visible police brutality against Black people. A new courtship during this time put us in a bubble, insulating us a bit from the madness. Our "bubble," as we came to call our courtship, felt safe. The conversations flowed freely, and all our dates reinforced our bubble concept because there were so few people around us. Our favorite date spots were outdoor rooftop restaurants in NYC. The skyline views were perfect and the spaces were practically empty due to COVID-19 protocols. You had to book a reservation well in advance and the capacity of the spaces were reduced to about ten people at a time. The few tables made available were spread to opposite sides of the roof. Tyrone and I could have an entire half of a rooftop to ourselves. We flirted and laughed like teenagers for hours. On one particular date, the emotional safety we created for each other allowed us to go from giggling to showing our scars. Tyrone's deep, smooth voice became barely audible as he spoke about his father for the first time. "I never really spent a lot of time with my dad growing up because he was away a lot; he pretty much belonged to the government."

My stomach dropped. I leaned in and grabbed his hand for support and immediately replied, "I understand. Having a loved one that's locked up is brutal. It's incredibly expensive to pay one dollar per minute to talk to the person you love on the phone. Driving in and out of state to see him through plexiglass is hell but it ain't much better sitting in a dirty visiting room in Rikers Island. But more than the money, prison robs us of having time and building memories with our family. That's the part that stays with us that we can never really shake. People should talk more openly about how difficult it is. How much time does he have left on his bid? I know it never gets easier—"

"SHANITA!" Tyrone interrupted me with a strange look on his face. "I never said my dad is in prison. Oh my God. I said he belongs to the government because he has a government job that always required him to work long hours."

After about a minute of awkward silence, I yelled, "Well

damn, nigga, stop using words like belonging to the government when you talking about Black men. That means prison!"

"Who does that mean prison to?" I could see him trying to process how I came to that conclusion. "Ohhhh, it's all the research you've been doing about incarceration for your fellowship and the criminal justice classes you teach. I get it." He nodded knowingly. "I think it's dope that you're so passionate about your work and you're always willing to teach people. I love that your mind is centered on issues like mass incarceration. It's part of why I like you so much." He gleamed at me with those dark piercing eyes and a soft smile.

I felt safe enough to tell him the truth about my ex-boyfriend, Anthony, and family members, but I didn't want to drift out of our bubble and start unpacking mass incarceration on a date night. The truth was whenever any Black person mentions "being away" in reference to relatives, I rarely ever think the person is on vacation. "Being away" is code for being incarcerated and ideas like "belong to the government" in reference to a Black person will NEVER make me think of employment. I was passionate about my career and mentally engulfed in research like Tyrone assumed, but I was also triggered by his choice of words and started to spiral.

I'd spent years supporting men I love through their incarcerations. The closer you are to the person who is incarcerated the more it feels like you are sentenced too. Nobody survives prison without trauma—no matter which side of the bars they are on.

I ultimately decided Tyrone and I made better sense as friends than lovers. We now have a casual friendship where we occasionally call each other, argue about something hip-hop related, or joke about life. He loves to tease me about the time I thought his father was in prison and says things like I don't like him because he's not "hood enough." I playfully agree with him and tell him that guys raised outside of the hood trigger me by using words like "government" and "away" in the same sentence. During one phone call I told him I once supported important people in my life through their incarceration. "Now I understand why you reacted that way when I told you my dad belonged to the government. Wow, so you're a real live ride-or-die chick, that's dope." For me it wasn't dope, and the joke deflated when Tyrone implied that it was.

Once again, he'd unintentionally affirmed my trauma. As a classic New York hip-hop head, Tyrone believed he was affirming me by calling me a ride-or-die chick—the ultimate title too many Black women are conditioned to strive for. He couldn't see the trauma in my response, but

I could. It felt easier to lean into his intentions than create another scene, so I responded, "Yeah, I am," and decided to let my trauma hide in plain sight. Most people are impacted by some form of traumatic experience. We all respond to our trauma in different ways, some of which are easy to miss or ignore. Identifying trauma responses can be complicated and typically requires peeling back emotional layers and sitting with some of the most painful experiences of your life. By no stretch of the imagination is it an easy process but it's impossible to heal without at least recognizing your trauma for what it is: trauma.

Not all of our trauma responses manifest in ways that are as lighthearted as my mishaps with Tyrone, nor are they as apparent as my anxiety about money. They can be convoluted, layered, and almost impossible to detect. They can be intertwined with positive attributes and behaviors. A special area of triumph and trauma that we must pay attention to in Black womanhood is Black motherhood. Listen to almost any hip-hop song that pays tribute to mothers and you will walk away with a common theme: Black mommas don't play about their kids! Some of my favorite songs are the ones rappers write about their relationships with their mothers. These loving tributes are often both an ode to their mothers and an indictment on an unfair system that created the conditions too many Black women are forced to raise children in.

Ghostface Killah does this masterfully in his song, "All That I Got Is You." In the song he's looking at the impossible situations his mother raised him in. *Eggs after school, eating grits 'cause we was poor...fifteen of us in a three-bedroom apartment.* He delves into the careless rule of the New York City Housing Authority that forces families out of their homes if a person living there is arrested and charged with a crime. The song also notes how social services workers can show disregard for their client's time. *Case worker had her runnin' back to face to face / I caught a case, housing tried to throw us out of our place.* His lyrics show his mother's tenderness in contrast to the brutal world she lived in. She licks her finger to gently smooth out his eyebrows on the way to school and asks their neighbors to borrow food to care for her family.

In "Dear Momma," Tupac sings about his mother being no stranger to raising her children against insurmountable odds. His mom was a master of magic math. She could turn a dollar into fifteen cents and would pretend she wasn't hungry just so her children wouldn't feel bad as she went without food to ensure they ate. Despite battling drug addiction, she reigned supreme in their home. According to Pac, *even as a crack fiend* she was still a *Black queen.*

Black mothers vary and not all of us share similar socioeconomic hardships or such a strong will, but we all know countless Black mothers who do. The Black mother archetype will do the impossible to protect and care for her children. The Black community is full of women doing the absolute most to protect their children. It is our norm and their love is beautiful and worthy of praise and these loving musical tributes. Yet since the notion of Black mothers defying limitations is a cultural norm, it can be difficult to identify when we've gone too far and end up harming the children we want to protect. Nothing blurs this line for me as a member of the Black mother tribe more than my inner struggle with feeling unprotected as a Black woman.

As a Black woman, the thought of my daughter ever feeling unprotected is triggering to me. When my daughter, Jordyn, shares an incident with me about somebody hurting her feelings or causing her harm in any way, it registers to me like a Bat-Signal and I swing into action ready to fight first and listen last. When Jordyn was in second grade, she came home repeating a phrase to me that almost made me toss my kitchen table over while we were eating dinner. I asked her if she wanted juice or water to drink and she said, "It doesn't matter, I'll get what I get and I won't complain." I had no idea where she learned that from, so I asked. She explained that her teacher said it to her every day in class so she could learn to become satisfied with whatever she was given. Before Jordyn got to

the end the story, I emailed the teacher to request a meeting and made a mental note to wear my sneakers and a
ponytail to her school—just in case. The next day I went
to the school and explained to her white teacher that I
won't allow her to teach my daughter to become a doc-
ile Negro just because that's the version of Blackness she
is most comfortable with. The teacher's eyes welled with
tears, mine inflamed with rage. She rationalized it by saying it was a phrase she repeated to the entire class so they
would stop squabbling over items she passed out. I told her
she was free to write her little mantra on a piece of paper
and pass it out to every other kid in that classroom, but
my child was to never hear those words again from her.
I continued with my history lesson on why white women
like her were dangerous to Black children and fortunately
for Jordyn she had a mother that would protect her at all
costs. It was a long meeting.

Jordyn never reported hearing those words again but
when she got older one day, she said something that stopped
me in my tracks: "Mom whenever I tell you something happened to me you blow up. You make it hard for me to tell
you stuff that happens to me because you always overreact.
It makes me feel like I can't talk to you even when I want
to." I was crushed. In my effort to make sure she always felt
protected I forgot to make sure she felt free. I prioritized

her feeling protected over anything else because I've always understood that one day, she will have to navigate life in a world that does not protect Black women.

Since the days of slavery, Black women have had to contend with medical racism. The "founding father" of gynecology, Dr. James Marion Sims, perfected his craft by performing operations on enslaved Black women without their consent or anesthesia. The false notion that Black women's bodies are not worthy of proper medical treatment and that we are too inhumane to feel pain was not eradicated when slavery ended.

As of 2020, research shows that "nearly a quarter of Black women between ages 18 and 30 have fibroids," but that Black women are also at least twice as likely as white women to have their uteruses removed through a hysterectomy. Doctors are recommending this drastic surgery to Black patients suffering from fibroids more often and more quickly than they do to white women. But the quantitative data that could speak to these racial disparities is lacking, which is a massive part of the problem. Black women are disproportionately afflicted with fibroids and undergoing hysterectomies at rates that surpass white women, but it isn't considered important enough to warrant significant funding and medical research. In 2019, data analysis from the American Journal of Emergency Medicine found that

Black patients were "40% less likely to receive medication for acute pain compared to white patients." The implication is that medical practitioners are less likely to listen to Black women when they are in pain, and thus, fibroids that could have easily been treated with less invasive measures (had they been identified earlier) are being treated with a hysterectomy.

Black women never needed quantitative data to confirm this. Too many of us have stories about being ignored by doctors, and it almost cost us our lives. In 2018, Serena Williams, the rich and world-renowned tennis player, almost died because she had to fight to make doctors listen to her about how she was feeling after giving birth. Experiencing medical racism is traumatic, but just knowing that you could be subject to subpar medical treatment because you're a Black woman is also traumatizing. Unfortunately this is not unique to the medical field, and racism isn't on hold until we turn eighteen. A report published by the Georgetown Law Center indicated that Black girls are perceived as "less innocent and more adult-like than white girls" and in need of less protection. In schools, this typically translates into Black girls receiving harsher punishments than white girls. From our ancestors to our childhood to adulthood, we navigate this world with less protection than white women. That is severely traumatic and it's manifesting in our lives. My response to constantly feeling unprotected can be found in my parenting style, but it's often mislabeled as "a Black momma not playing about her kid." Meanwhile, my daughter suffers the repercussions of not feeling free enough to share more things with me because I could lose it or blow up, therefore conditioning her to remain silent about her pain. Misidentified trauma responses have to be recognized and continuously worked on to be healed.

One of the greatest threats to the well-being of Black women is not recognizing behaviors as trauma responses, because it keeps us trapped in a dangerous cycle of self-harm. We are definitely susceptible to this when our trauma responses coincide with practices that we value and honor, and that we are praised and celebrated for in our culture and music. The validation makes it easier to not address the issue, which only allows the trauma to swell and win us over. But peel back the layers of your response when it is overwhelming, and find where it may be connected to a specific trauma. Therapy provides tools for this healing journey, but it's a journey we don't have to take alone. Before she died, bell hooks said, "Rarely, if ever, are any of us healed in isolation. Healing is an act of communion."

She understood that healing is a community response. We heal together by trusting each other enough to bring our hurts to the forefront and share our truths. We lovingly call each other in when we see these trauma responses and do as bell instructed, heal in community.

ACKNOWLEDGMENTS

It takes a village to raise an author, and the Spirit of God to select your village. I am forever thankful to God and my village. Jordyn, you are my everything. From the moment I found out I was pregnant, you have been my inspiration. Twelve years later and you still inspire me. Thank you for believing in this book and for being so understanding when I spent countless hours bringing it to life. I hope it makes you proud. Mom, you are my everything. Thank you for pushing me to dream big and for always being there to give me wings. To my brothers, I love you all. Nakia Oliver, I am who I am because of you; Jerome Hubbard, you are my heart; and Matthew Carroll, you are forever my favorite little brother. To my "soul mates," I don't ever want to imagine a life without any of you. Chevyonne Dillon, Latonia Dillon, and Genelle Barksdale—from "sand park" to infinity, it's always been us, and will forever be us. Oh and for the love of God, Nellie stop asking me about that damn 112 CD.

To the Degree and Oliver squad, next to good health there is nothing better than a loving family. Thanks for being a solid foundation. I love you all. Yenny, Toone, and Miriam "Titi" Lopez, I am so honored that God hand selected you both to be my sisters and prayer partners. Titi, your words helped me finish this book when I started to doubt, and Yen, as always you were my rock. Davita McKelvey, who knew our relationship would take so many shapes over the years?! Even when we are millions of miles apart you are always by my side. Rosalind Lucien, I might owe you an apology. I'm pretty certain God moved you to your current city because he knew I would need you. Thank you for being my friend, holding down Jordyn so I could write, and sharing your amazing daughter with me.

Thank you to my squad of dope ass writers, David Dennis Jr., Bee Quammie, Dara Mathis, Nubyjas Wilborn, Shameka Irby, Vann Newkirk, and of course Garfield Hylton, the genius who brought us all together. We started out as just a bunch of Black writers supporting each other and gradually we turned into family. Thank y'all for always supporting me and this book. I love y'all forever and ever. To my work husband, Jay Connor, I am forever thankful for you, love you always.

To my agent, William LoTurco, thank you for believing in me from day one. To my book editor Krishan Trotman, you might not even realize it but there were moments where I had to borrow some of the faith you had in me. Thanks for taking great care with me and my book baby, we did it!

When you're a freelance writer, the editors you work with shape you in profound ways. Thank you to every editor who I ever worked with. I appreciate you giving me a shot and pushing me to be a better writer. To the Black women who did this work long before me so that this book can even exist, I thank you immensely. Where would I be without my beloved HBCU? Thank you to my MoCo family. I love you forever. Finally, I am forever thankful for the city that raised me. Y.O., home of the brave.

One final note, as I write this, it's officially two days before your funeral and I will never get to hear your thoughts about this book but I know you would've been proud. RIP Uncle Al, pour one out with Uncle Clyde when you see him.